CRUISE

CONTROL

A Complete Guide

to

Carefree Cruising

Robin Gail

DISCLAIMER

Not every tip or suggestion in this book will apply to every cruise ship. Many of the tips are generic to ships in general.

While the author has been on many cruises, she has not been on every cruise ship on the seas.

The author has made every attempt to provide accuracy of the content herein.

The author does not assume any liability to any person for loss, damage, or disruption caused by the suggestions made in this book or caused by errors or omissions.

There are no affiliate links in this book. Nor is the author associated with any cruise line mentioned in this book.

COPYRIGHT

The information in this book contains the opinions and ideas of the author.

No part of this book may be reproduced, stored in a retrieval system or database, or transmitted in any form by any means, electronic, mechanical, photocopied, recorded, scanning, or otherwise without the prior written consent of the publisher except brief quotations contained within reviews.

The author is not affiliated in any way with any cruise line mentioned in this book.

Copyright 2019 by Robin Gail. All rights reserved. Printed in the United States of America.

Cover design by Wageedah Salie, One Story Creative

www.onestorycreative.net

ISBN 978-0-9992476-8-6

Contents

INTRODUCTION 1

Chapter 1 - PLANNING YOUR CRUISE 11
   A.   WHICH SIZE SHIP? 11
   B.   APPS 12
   C.   ARE CRUISES ALL-INCLUSIVE? 15
   D.   ARE YOU SAFE AT SEA? 17
   E.   DEPARTURE PORTS 19
   F.   YOUR SHIPBOARD ACCOUNT & CRUISE CARD .. 19
   G.   WHERE DO YOU WANT TO CRUISE? 22
   H.   WHEN DO YOU WANT TO CRUISE? 28
   I.   CRUISING SOLO 30
   J.   CABINS & CABIN BATHROOMS 33
   K.   CRUISE TERMINOLOGY 48
   L.   PORTS OF CALL & EXCURSIONS 53
   M.   PASSPORTS & PRE-CRUISE DOCUMENTS 64
   N.   SAVE MONEY WHEN BOOKING YOUR CRUISE .. 68
   O.   TRAVEL INSURANCE 76
   P.   WHERE DO CREW MEMBERS/STAFF MEMBERS LIVE? 78

Chapter 2 - PACKING TIPS & HINTS 81
   A.   DON'T FORGET THESE 81
   B.   LEAVE THESE AT HOME 104

Chapter 3 – EMBARKATION DAY/BOARDING 109
   A.   ARRIVING AT THE PORT 109
   B.   WHAT TO BRING IN CARRY-ON BAG 113

- C. BOARDING THE SHIP 116
- D. ON-BOARD PHOTOS 120

Chapter 4 – LIFE ON BOARD THE SHIP 123
- A. DRESS 123
- B. KIDS' CLUBS 129
- C. CELL PHONES 131
- D. FREEBIES & DISCOUNTS 132
- E. DRINK PACKAGES & ON-BOARD BEVERAGES . 141
- F. DINING ON BOARD 144
- G. CHOOSE TO BE CONSIDERATE 149
- H. THINGS TO DO ON BOARD YOUR SHIP 158
- I. GRATUITIES & TIPPING 170
- J. THANK YOUR CABIN STEWARD 174

Chapter 5 – DEBARKATION 179
- A. SETTLING YOUR ON-BOARD ACCOUNT 179
- B. DEBARKATION OF LUGGAGE 179
- C. DEBARKATION OF PASSENGERS 181

CONCLUSION 185

AUTHOR'S REQUEST 187

ABOUT THE AUTHOR 189

REFERENCES 191

INTRODUCTION

Looking for the ins and outs of a cruise vacation? You've come to the right place! Cruises rock! They are our favorite way to vacation.

This book will take the overwhelm out of planning a cruise for you and your family. You will find excellent cruise tips, tricks, and hacks sure to make your experience more delightful!

Exotic, beautiful ports, delicious food (at any time of the day or night), a ship full of friendly people, wonderful Broadway-style shows, game shows, contests, parades, karaoke, sports, beautiful sparkling pools!

Not sure if you honestly want to take a cruise? This book is loaded with information certain to help you decide. I promise your cruise experience will be much better and much less overwhelming if you are prepared, especially if this is your first cruise.

This must-read book will make you one of the most informed passengers on the ship! Glance at the *Table of Contents* to see all it has to offer.

Get ready to de-stress and leave your worries and troubles at home! You know what the real world is, right? Well, your cruise begins your fantasy world for the entirety of your trip.

You will be so relaxed as you take in the views, the many diverse cultures, the exquisite and mouthwatering cuisine, and the sheer beauty of our world. The emotional benefit you will sense is exhilarating!

I have not filled this book with pictures because you can google any cruise ship and see pictures of the ship for yourself. You can also find plenty of YouTube videos taken by cruisers who are happy to share their experience, including their cabins, via video.

I believe the ideal way to have a successful cruise experience is through *great preparation*. My hope is this book will help you prepare so there's nothing left to do but have fun!

After all, you don't want to learn *on* your first cruise, you want to learn *before* your first cruise!

Cruising does not *have* to be expensive. Let me show you how you can save!

Remember when cruising was for couples or older folks, not families (Disney Cruise Lines comes

INTRODUCTION

to mind)? Remember when it cost an arm and a leg to go on a cruise? Not so anymore! Read on, friends!

Your cruise fare can be all-inclusive. In fact, you can get transportation to and from the airport to the pier included in your fare. How convenient is that!?

You can have your alcohol and soft drinks, even flights included in your total fare.

Cruising can be costly, or cruising can be a reasonable vacation. It is what you make it. It can be all-inclusive, or you can add expenses such as liquor, excursions, and specialty restaurants. Read on, and I'll explain.

New, bigger, fancier ships come on the scene frequently. Does not mean you need to take one of those higher priced ones! We know there's fun to be found on all ships!

If you are looking to save money on your dream vacation while still getting the most from your trip, I have a chapter with tips on freebies and discounts! Who doesn't want to save money on the cost of a vacation? Frugal cruising is a possibility!

We have met older cruisers who have chosen to live out the rest of their days living on a ship. Can

Cruise Control

you believe it is less expensive to retire and enjoy a cruise every week than live at assisted living?

If you're one of the many fortunate elderly who is in reasonably good health, why not give it a go!? Pretty much everything is done for you on a ship! And there's a doctor and medical clinic a couple of minutes away.

If you have special needs and want to take a cruise, you will find the ships try in every way possible to accommodate you. There are cabins specifically for people with disabilities or special needs. I would advise you to book these cabins early.

Do keep in mind while you are on board, no equipment whatsoever, such as wheelchairs, is allowed to be stored out in the hallways.

You will find this type of information on the cruise line's website. If you have a need for something not listed on their site, it's a phone call away. They will be happy to assist you in any way possible!

You will find age groups from babies (not all ships), toddlers, teens, all the way to seasoned cruisers in their 90s.

INTRODUCTION

Cruising is endless fun for people of all ages. It is a vacation where the children can go have their separate fun, the adults can go have their separate fun, and yet, everyone can come together to make it a great family vacation.

Ponder a vacation where all you will have to make a decision about is where you will eat or what show you want to go see. Oh, you may have to decide which excursion you want to go on too!

I try to provide you the best cruise hacks and even secrets we have found in our years of enjoying this type of vacationing.

I am here to help you get the most from your cruise vacation. You will find tips galore here!

There is no right or wrong way to enjoy a cruise vacation, but with these tips, you will have a head start to fun.

This book is great for newbie cruisers and seasoned cruisers as well. It is designed to help you have a smooth, stress-free, and enjoyable cruise!

Cruising is a wonderful experience you may not be able to get the full effect of if you don't have some tips, tricks and information ahead of time.

Cruise Control

Get ready to be pampered on your cruise. You will be, from the beginning to the end.

Are you afraid of the seas? There is Wi-Fi, cell phone service, satellite TV, doctors and other medical personnel on all ships. You are not alienated from existence. No matter what the emergency may be, there is a way to be safe.

Though I know they exist, we have never seen an emergency while at sea.

If there is any type of emergency involving the ship such as rough seas, Norovirus (ugh), etcetera, please take care of the children first. We all know little ones are at the mercy of adults to keep them safe.

So maybe you're not afraid of the open seas but you are claustrophobic. Don't let it hinder you! You will find open air all over the ship!

Many of the ships have entirely open-air centers. These open-air promenades are four, five, six or more stories high. This is normally called the Boardwalk area and is filled with shops.

Go to the top of the ship and you'll have all the space you need! Plus, the theaters and restaurants are huge!

INTRODUCTION

Perhaps you do not like crowds. You will find a lot of space on a cruise ship where you can be alone. Passengers are so spread out on ships, the likelihood of having a bout of claustrophobia is small.

While ships are extremely safe, please remember they are huge, floating cities. Accidents and emergencies do happen. Security is constantly on alert for this.

But use your common sense, exactly like you would do at home.

Depending on the length of your cruise, you can see a large amount of the world in a small amount of time with as much or as little activity as you desire.

Cruising offers you the chance to see the diversity of our world and its people, all while relaxing on a beautiful, floating resort while sampling exquisite cuisine from all around the world.

You will find different cruise lines specialize in different categories of people. For example, different age groups.

Many people want quieter ships or ships which cater to older cruisers, while others want party ships.

Cruise Control

Research each cruise line independently on-line if you are concerned about this. There is a wealth of information on the Internet for each cruise line and their ships and activities on board.

Whatever cruise line you are choosing to travel with, be sure to check their website for any kind of restrictions on luggage, what you can bring on board, etcetera.

As you start your voyage, be open to meeting new people and having new experiences. You will undoubtedly do both.

Oftentimes, people will meet for the first time on the first day or two and hang out together for the duration of their cruise. Other times, you may want to enjoy the ones you are cruising with.

You or someone you love having a birthday or anniversary while you are on board? Every cruise line we have been on allows you to pre-order flowers, chocolates, or gifts before your trip even begins!

Look at your cruise line's website at all they have to offer for those special occasions. What a wonderful surprise to walk into your cabin and find a huge bouquet of flowers (chocolate for me) sitting there from your loved one!

Your choices are endless to enjoy your vacation the way you want to. You get to do exactly what you wish to do. You get to control how your day will be. You can relax all day or stay busy from waking till bedtime.

We know for sure you will never get bored! Enjoy your vacation of a lifetime on your own floating, breathtaking city!

Savor every moment of your journey while you break away from your daily routine and let someone else pamper you!

So excited for you to begin your journey! My hope for you is that with the help of this book, you will be one of the most informed guests on your ship!

Wishing you a marvelous time on your cruise!

Bon voyage!

Chapter 1 - PLANNING YOUR CRUISE

A. WHICH SIZE SHIP?

I truly believe we have cruised on every size ship on the seas, smallest to largest.

If you get on a ship you are not comfortable with, it could impact the fun of your trip! Something we do not want to happen!

I'll share with you what we've learned over the years about the different cruise lines and various ships.

On our last cruise, we were on one of the largest ships at sea (over 6k passengers). And honestly, we have decided those huge ships are not for us. But they are for tons of cruisers! We prefer the mid-size ships (3k-4k).

Truthfully, the hustle and bustle is not what bothers us. You will see hustle and bustle on all size ships. The amount of human traffic is what we like to keep lower (the 3k-4k).

You are able to find many peace and quiet places, even on the largest of ships. We have always seen *adults only* areas, often called Serenity, on every large ship we've been on. And we have taken advantage of it!

You will find the same kinds of activities, fun, and shows on both large and mid-size ships. The only difference is there will be fewer people participating in the activities, so more space for you to participate!

We enjoy seeing the same people when we cruise and have become friends with fellow cruisers due to running into them frequently. You may not get this opportunity on those huge ships.

You will, of course, have more walking on the giant ships. We don't necessarily mind the walking, but it cuts into our fun time!

Every venue on the ship will be less crowded on the mid-size ships. We have discovered we like this.

B. APPS

When trying to decide which cruise line you want to cruise with or which ship you want to cruise on, go on-line and read some of the passenger reviews.

An excellent source for reviews of ships is www.cruisemates.com.

Chapter 1 - PLANNING YOUR CRUISE

Remember, though, some people live *negatively* and will complain about every little thing. Thus, a negative review gets left for the ship. Others will be open-minded and assume people are looking for honest reviews.

One of the first things you may want to do after you have made the decision to take a cruise is download the free (at time of this writing) app, Cruise Ship Mate.

This app has a fun-to-watch countdown to your cruise. Says it works for any cruise line. You will get all kinds of information on this app, even setting it for price alerts.

If the cruise price goes down, you will be notified. How awesome is that!?

This app has deck plans and ship information for most ships. It has excursion options listed as well as a chat option for other cruisers on your ship. It has forums for people to share their knowledge and tips about cruising. Plus, a whole lot more!

Most all of the cruise lines have apps providing all sorts of pertinent information. Excursions, shopping, ship tracking, port information. The apps also have a place for you to store your photos.

Cruise Control

Should you lose your camera or phone, you'll still have your photos.

You'll find most anything you need to know about your ship on their app. You will find the ship's activities as well as their restaurants and other important information.

You can even book your appointments on their app such as dinner at specialty restaurants and treatments in the spa.

A free app called My Data Manager will help you with tracking your usage on your cell phone. It has a custom alert to let you know if you have other items running in the background which may be using your data.

Check out XE Currency, also free. This one helps you figure out exchange rates in other countries.

Research this before you leave home, and it will save the latest rates on your phone so you do not have to use the Internet on board your ship.

There is an app called Cruise Card Control which helps you budget and track your on-board spending.

Another useful and free app is Mobile Passport. Enter your information on this app, and you will be able to skip the long lines at customs.

There is customarily a line marked Mobile Passport at the U.S. Customs' counter.

C. ARE CRUISES ALL-INCLUSIVE?

The price of your cruise generally includes the port taxes or port charges. The individual governments of the ports you visit may have minimal additional government taxes or port taxes, so you may see these occasionally but rarely.

The cruise ports your ship visits will charge the cruise line for every passenger on board the ship. This is the port charge or tax.

If you ask your travel agent or cruise agent, you should be able to get the total price of your cruise, including the above-mentioned fees.

Though the price of a cruise is all-inclusive, extras such as shore excursions, Kids' Clubs (some, not all), alcohol, specialty dining (not the main dining room), and spa treatments are not included in the cost. You may want to consider this as you are planning your cruise.

Cruise Control

There are casual restaurants on board included in your cost as well. There are a variety of choices aside from the specialty restaurants.

You'll see people choosing not to do any of these extra-cost festivities and merely enjoy the ride and fun.

In our experience, the following are extras we have found to cost over and above the cost of your cruise. Most are at your discretion.

- tipping
- gambling
- purchases in any of the on-board shops
- professional photographs
- alcohol, soft drinks, specialty coffees
- medical treatment (However, we required medical treatment on our last cruise due to my husband getting stitches in his hand injured while playing dodgeball and the clinic did not charge us as they said the accident occurred while participating in on-board activity.)
- shore excursions
- spa treatments
- travel insurance
- laundry services

Chapter 1 - PLANNING YOUR CRUISE

- Internet and cell usage
- bingo
- airfare (if you do not live in a port city)

And, of course, there may be other expenses we have not had or heard about.

D. ARE YOU SAFE AT SEA?

We've been on over 25 cruises and have never, not one time, felt unsafe. We have never been scared or had any feeling of trepidation at all.

Cruise ships adhere to strict security measures and guidelines.

See the U.S. Coast Guard's Security for Passenger Vessels and Passenger Terminals regulations. This is too lengthy to put in this book, but I will quickly go over several points.

Ships will sometimes have an armed escort out of ports by the U.S. Coast Guard. People tend to capture pictures of this from the top decks on sail-away.

There are several points of entry on ships with access entirely controlled by security. Not a single person can board a ship without proper

Cruise Control
===

identification and without going through metal detectors.

The identification gets scanned through the scanner which holds the ship's manifest. *Every* person is accounted for.

Oftentimes, you will likely pass through three to four security checkpoints before boarding your ship, including the port terminal of the area you may be visiting.

Every item put on the ship is sent through security screening and X-rayed, including all luggage and carry-on luggage and all cargo. To avoid any delay, you may want to unlock your luggage before handing it over to porters.

There are highly-trained security personnel, including former military and naval personnel, on every cruise ship as well as surveillance cameras monitoring every public area of the ship.

In addition, there is a large security zone around ships. No private watercraft is allowed to come within the no-float zone.

Again, if you are skeptical about safety, please google the information for safety aboard ships cruising all over the world.

E. DEPARTURE PORTS

If you are boarding the ship from an out-of-town port, it is advisable to book your flight for the previous day and get a hotel room near the port the ship is leaving from so you will not miss the ship.

You never know what might happen at an airport. Flight delays, misplaced luggage, etcetera. And the ship will most likely not wait for you to get there.

Most hotels near cruise ports will provide free or discounted transportation to and from the pier.

F. YOUR SHIPBOARD ACCOUNT & CRUISE CARD

All ships use a cashless system. When you book your cruise, you provide a credit card number which will hold all of the purchases you make on board and your expenses.

If you do not have any credit cards, you are able to provide cash in lieu of a credit card. If you are using strictly cash for expenses on your trip, you will receive an explanation for how to do this.

As you board your ship, you will be issued a Sail & Sign card, or what some refer to as a cruise card,

Cruise Control

connected to your credit card number. You will receive this cruise card before you board the ship.

All charges on your ship board account will be put on this cruise card. You will receive your itemized bill of your ship charges at the end of your trip.

The bill will be paid by the credit card or cash you provided when you booked your cruise.

Before you leave home, you may want to notify your credit card companies of your plans to travel. They sometimes freeze accounts or put holds on accounts if there is unusual activity far from where you live.

You are able to check your statement or itemized bill on your cabin television. This is a great convenience as people do not know, may not realize or may forget how much extra they are spending.

I advise checking your bill every night when you retire for the evening. We have found errors on our statements more than once. If you find an error, go to the Guest Services' desk to settle it.

At the end of your voyage, if your itemized account statement looks accurate, you are good to go. No need to do anything else as it will be charged

Chapter 1 - PLANNING YOUR CRUISE

to the credit card you provided when you booked your cruise.

These cruise cards are called by different names by each of the various cruise lines. It functions the same though.

It is your cabin door key, your credit card for on-board purchases, and you will be required to show this card every time you leave the ship or get back on the ship.

This is how they make sure all cruisers are back on the ship at a port.

Be careful with your card. Keep it away from magnets and cell phones. You may deactivate it if you don't. If this happens to you, the front desk will issue you another card in a matter of minutes. No worries!

If you lose this card, report it *immediately*. Anyone else can use it. The front desk is able to cancel your lost card and quickly replace it.

If you do not have any credit cards, you will be able to open a cash account with a certain amount of cash per person. The cash will be put on your cruise card. If you do not spend all of the cash you put down, of course you will receive your cash back.

<u>Cruise Control</u>

If you go over your cash limit, you will have to pay the balance before you leave the ship.

Be sure you know what you are paying for and how much you are spending. When you book your cruise, whether on-line or through a travel agent, make certain to read all the fine print.

You won't experience sticker shock when your dream vacation is over if you have read the fine print!

G. WHERE DO YOU WANT TO CRUISE?

Please keep in mind, this information is at the time of this particular writing and may be subject to change at any moment.

Caribbean cruises are typically four nights or longer, cruising to many islands in the Caribbean. Expect sun and fun, beautiful beaches, excellent shopping, and history in these ports.

Caribbean cruises depart from Texas, Florida, Louisiana, Alabama, New York, and Puerto Rico. The best time to visit the Caribbean is December to March as it is not too hot during this time.

Chapter 1 - PLANNING YOUR CRUISE

However, school is out in some of this time (holidays, spring breaks), so you may find the ships crowded.

Are you interested in gambling? You'll find it in the Bahamas along with sun and beautiful beaches. Parasailing, jet skiing, beach volleyball, snorkeling, scuba diving and loads of other activities are plentiful.

Alaska cruises are at least seven days, most often several days longer. These cruises sail from San Francisco, Seattle, Anchorage, and Vancouver. You will see breathtaking sites including glaciers, snow-covered mountains, whales, and quaint towns, to name a few.

Alaska is one of the most beautiful places we've cruised to. You will see places you can only see by cruise ship.

When we sailed to Alaska, there were places on the ship so quiet you could hear a pin drop! Everyone was in total awe of this gorgeous state!

The season for Alaskan cruises is from early May to September. You may be able to find some repositioning cruises in the September and October time frame as Alaska's season will be over, and the ship's will be relocating.

Hibernation is over around the end of summer, so if wildlife interests you, cruising then is best.

Towards the end of summer, you will find tremendous savings at the shops as the merchants are trying to sell everything before they close for the winter months.

The Mediterranean is known for its historical and cultural interests. Heard of the Mediterranean diet? This is some of the healthiest and most delicious cuisine in the world.

The high season for this area is May to September. You will see lots of families cruising during their summer vacations.

At the time of this writing, these cruises depart from Spain, Italy, Greece, and Turkey.

Antarctica is simply beautiful. Watching the beautiful mountains while floating on water as crystal clear as glass is breathtaking. You will likely see penguins in this area as well as whales surfacing.

Chapter 1 - PLANNING YOUR CRUISE

You will only be able to cruise this area during November to March. Departure is from Argentina, Chile, and New Zealand.

You'll find longer voyages in Africa. You will cruise along both the east and west coastlines, capturing beautiful sites.

You may see various wildlife in this area right from your ship. Don't forget the Nile River and the pyramids if you love history.

You'll depart from Egypt, Morocco, and South Africa.

Prepare for 10-day to 14-day voyages to the Panama Canal. Quiet cruises with interesting, rich history elements to them.

If you are looking for natural wonders, you'll want to consider cruising in the Australia/New Zealand region.

Snorkeling around the Great Barrier Reef is a visitor favorite. You'll see pristine white beaches, breathtaking waterfalls, and beautiful rainforests.

Cruises in this area depart from Sydney, Brisbane, Adelaide, and Auckland and run year-round with peak season from October to April.

Cruise Control

If you are cruising from the United States during the winter, it will be Australia's summer. Head there if you dislike winter (like me).

Canada/New England's cruise season is from May to October. It will be hot and humid in mid-summer and chilly toward the end of the season.

The small towns welcome cruisers, giving a big welcoming party for the ships. You will find beautiful foliage, sandy beaches, and friendly people there.

Northern Europe's busy season for cruising is June to September. The locals love to be outdoors.

Cruise fares to Europe tend to be lower in spring and fall. Beautiful sunsets abound in this area. You will see architectural treasures boasting interesting history.

Medieval structures, castles and cathedrals are plentiful. Museums and tours abound in this beautiful area.

Bermuda is known for its gorgeous pink sand and blue water. It also has great shopping. Or how about caverns with a floating pathway guests walk on? You'll see beautiful limestone formations as well.

Chapter 1 - PLANNING YOUR CRUISE

If you are interested in rain forests and lots of wildlife, South America cruises are for you. The beautiful Andes Mountains are in this region, as well as interesting history and cultures.

These cruises are typically 12 days to 17 days long. Busy season is typically November through March.

South Pacific cruises are longer cruises, ordinarily more than 10 days. The areas are beautiful. Fiji, Australia and New Zealand, Tahiti, Hawaii.

Hawaii's busy season is December until May. Air travel can be expensive during this time. The weather is typically hot and humid.

Rainy season is from December to March.

Every island is a different experience from partying on Honolulu to the quietness on Maui. If snorkeling, water skiing, beautiful beaches, and volcanoes interest you, head to Hawaii. The Pacific Ocean is beautiful!

Wherever you choose to cruise in this vast, beautiful world, you will have experiences unlike any you've ever had.

H. WHEN DO YOU WANT TO CRUISE?

January and February can be better months to book a cruise. Why? We are coming off the holiday season and people are not generally thinking of a cruise.

Prices tend to be lower during this time as well. The kids are back in school after the holidays, so there will likely be less of them on the ship (just an FYI in case you are averse to kids).

Personally, I love watching the little ones on cruises having so much fun while they give their parents a little break!

If you are looking for sandy beaches with snorkeling, keep in mind the Caribbean water tends to be chilly during the beginning of the year. As we get into March and April, the waters are beginning to warm.

In April, the prices will be heading on an upward trend. The busy season is coming, and ships are repositioning during this time. Options for sailing are less which drives the cost of a cruise higher. Prices will likely continue to climb thereafter.

You should book your cruise for May early, as this is when people are ready to hit the beaches. School years end around the middle to end of May, so

Chapter 1 - PLANNING YOUR CRUISE

families will be planning to take their vacations during the summer months. Get a head start, and plan your cruise early.

Peak sailing for cruise ships is June and July. Families have three months to get those summer vacations in. Consequently, prices will be higher. Doesn't seem fair, I know. But that's the way it is.

As school begins to be in session again towards the end of August, you will see the price of cruises drop a bit. This is the beginning of hurricane season, however, so you will want to keep this in mind as you plan your voyage.

Most all of our cruises have been during this time period, as our anniversary is in September. I can honestly tell you we have been in a storm only one time. And it was not frightening at all!

In September, hurricane season is in full force. But you will find some unbelievable bargains! Also, this is right after the new school year begins in certain places, and parents are less likely to take their kids out of school for a family vacation.

October is a great time to book transatlantic cruises. These are customarily 14 days or longer, so plan accordingly. Instead of stopping at ports daily, these types of cruises have more days at sea for those of you who love to kick back and relax on the ship.

Cruise prices will be higher in December during holiday season. However, the first two weeks of December are less expensive than the last two weeks. The ships will be less crowded the first two weeks.

A rule of thumb is to remember cruises are less expensive when children are in school. The cruise lines are trying to fill their ships.

Most cruise lines reposition their ships at some point during the year. Repositioning cruises are offered at large discounts. They are essentially trying to cover their cost. Yet you are still offered all the amenities of a full-price cruise.

I. CRUISING SOLO

A cruise taken solo could be the most amazing trip of all! You will find numerous activities on board for single people as well as those traveling alone.

Because you are traveling alone does not mean you truly are alone. Most people on cruise ships are super friendly. And many, like me, enjoy talking to people.

Chapter 1 - PLANNING YOUR CRUISE

If you choose to, you will likely meet people who are cruising solo like you are!

Most cruise ships have a Meet and Greet for singles on the first or second night. What a great way to meet fellow travelers who may be cruising alone!

Cabin prices are based on double occupancy, so some cruise lines charge a surcharge if you are traveling solo. Perhaps you could find a friend or family member to go with you. You may pay less.

On specific cruise lines, you will find studio cabins designed for one person. Holland America, Norwegian, and Royal Caribbean to name a few.

If you are traveling solo, you may want to book early as these cabins are not plentiful and tend to fill fast.

One of the perks of traveling alone is you get to do whatever you want when you want to do it. If you've always wanted to scuba dive but didn't because a significant other was with you, do it now!

You may see solo travelers book excursions with other travelers from the ship. Great way to get to know people!

Cruise Control

Safety needs to be your primary concern if you are traveling solo. Make sure your cell phone is in working order at all times. Some travelers have a GPS they like to use on their phone.

Be sure to leave a copy of your documents, including a copy of your passport and itinerary of your trip, at home with loved ones.

Keep in touch with your loved ones back home, especially if you are close to your family. You do not want to needlessly worry them.

Do not lower your guard if you are traveling alone. Don't get distracted. It is always best to know your surroundings and be safe, even on a cruise.

If you need to ask a question in port, it is preferable to ask someone in a shop, not a person walking on the street.

It is a good idea to keep your identification, money, and your cell phone on your person (in your pockets) while you are in ports. We have seen others who have left their bag in a restaurant in port, unable to get it back.

Write the name of your ship on a piece of paper and put the paper in your pocketbook.

Whether cruising solo or not, please do not try to get too cozy with a crew member. This is unacceptable to the cruise line and could cause the staff member to lose their job! Don't tempt them!

J. CABINS & CABIN BATHROOMS

There are four types of cabins on a ship. Inside, outside, balcony, and suite. We've tried them all, so I will share with you what we've learned.

When you book your cruise, you may have the option of a To-Be-Assigned cabin. This will get you a better cabin at a lesser price. They will pick the cabin out for you. If your travel agent forgets to mention this, ask them.

There is sometimes substantial savings if you are willing to let the cruise line pick your cabin out for you.

More times than not, we have met people who got a to-be-assigned cabin, and they were extremely happy with it!

Some of these cabins will have what is called an "obstructed view." This means you may be looking out of your window at lifeboats or some other type of equipment.

Cruise Control

Or they may be in a less desired area of the ship, such as above the Lido deck (where the noisy buffets are located).

And at time of boarding, you can ask to be upgraded to a better cabin at no charge.

A large number of cruise lines are now offering what is called Studio cabins. These are smaller cabins, accommodating one person. If you are traveling alone, this might be ideal for you! Do your due diligence and compare prices.

There is one advantage to these tiny cabins. Some ships with these cabins have a studio-only lounge with snacks and drinks which is another great way to meet others who may be traveling solo.

When booking your cabin, consider whether you will want a view or not. For instance, cruises to Alaska and Hawaii will have gorgeous, breathtaking views.

If you're not concerned with views, book an inside stateroom. These are considerably more economical.

An inside cabin is extremely small. But remember, most people are rarely in their cabin anyway. These are located in the inside wall of the

Chapter 1 - PLANNING YOUR CRUISE

corridors. These rooms have no windows. However, you can turn your television to the ship's bridge cam to know when it is light outside.

Again, if you do not mind having no window, this is, by far, the most economical way to cruise. These cabins are typically in the range of 150 square feet, give or take.

Some inside cabins have huge virtual screens continually playing beautiful scenes. Helps to keep cabin fever at bay.

Outside cabins with portholes or windows allow you to have a view of the ocean. No balcony though. These cabins are nice, in the range of about 200 square feet.

If you are booking a cabin with a window, keep in mind the cabins on the lower levels will have a porthole for a window, not a full-size window.

Balcony cabins are larger than a window cabin. Have your beverage sitting on your private balcony and enjoy watching the ocean and maybe dolphins, flying fish, or whales.

There are partitions on each side of the balcony, so your privacy is guaranteed.

Cruise Control

Balcony rooms and junior suites are able to accommodate three or four guests. You will be able to make the sofa into a bed or push two twin beds together to make a full-size bed. You can also ask for a rollaway bed.

You most always pay less for the third and fourth person in the same cabin.

We have seen cruise lines offer the third and fourth person free, especially for children. You likely will not see this offer during peak cruising season.

If you intend to have more than two people in your cabin, be sure to ask for one large enough to accommodate everyone in the cabin.

There are people who prefer to spend much of their time in their room, reading or relaxing. I suggest a cabin with a balcony if this is the case.

When searching for a cabin to book, you may notice the balcony cabins are different sizes. Oftentimes, the larger balcony cabins are not much more expensive than the smaller balcony cabin. They sometimes have a larger balcony as well.

Some ships, especially on river cruises, have French balconies. You can open your cabin door, but

Chapter 1 - PLANNING YOUR CRUISE

there is nowhere to sit. There is a railing there but nowhere to put chairs.

In other words, you cannot walk out onto a balcony, but you are able to open your cabin door all the way.

Royal Caribbean (I am unaware if other cruise lines have these cabins yet) has cabins facing the Boardwalk or Promenade area. This is through the center of the ship. These cabins have bay windows overlooking the Promenade.

We have never stayed in a cabin of this type, but we've been told cruisers love them. If you love people watching, keep your curtains open and watch away! I'd keep those curtains close in the evenings though.

The suites are the cabins with the most luxury. Some have separate living areas. The balcony on these suites is large, as are the bathrooms.

If you book an owner's suite or the equivalent type suite, you may have a Happy Hour with free cocktails and hors d'oeuvres included with your cost. This is one of the perks of booking the higher-priced rooms.

<u>Cruise Control</u>

You may also receive perks for the spa and special dining options. The suites are customarily located on the top floors of the ship.

If you are traveling with a family, it is likely less expensive to book two adjoining rooms instead of a suite.

The dividers on some of the balcony rooms will open to the neighbor's balcony to make it much larger. You will need to speak with your steward about this, however, as sometimes it is prohibited to open the dividers.

Some cruisers will book their older children's interior cabin across the hall from the adult balcony room. Excellent way to save money. There are some cruise lines who do not allow this though. They want the kids' cabin connected to the adults' cabin.

When booking your cruise, if you are booking two rooms with the intent of putting your teenage children in one, you will want to book the cruise with one adult in each room. This will let the cruise line know you are being responsible with your teens.

After sailing, if you are comfortable with it, let the teens have one room, adults have the other.

Chapter 1 - PLANNING YOUR CRUISE

Often, you can find videos on YouTube of the cabins of the cruise line you are cruising with. These videos are super informative. We generally view our cabin on YouTube before we book the cruise.

If you are convinced the motion of the ship (which you will rarely, if ever, feel) will disturb your sleep, choose a cabin more towards the center of the ship.

From personal experience, I can tell you the places NOT to book your stateroom. Read on.

One of the biggest mistakes we've made on a cruise is booking a cabin right below the Lido deck.

The Lido deck (top deck) is where the buffet is located as well as late-night deck parties. You may hear the clanging of dishes late at night and early in the morning. You may hear the music from the DJ or band late at night.

Avoid booking a cabin near any public area, either above it or below it.

If possible, try not to book a cabin directly above or below a public restroom. You may hear doors opening and shutting as well as loud hand dryers.

Cruise Control

When looking at the map of the ship on-line, it can sometimes be tricky to figure out where public restrooms are located. You can count on public restrooms being outside the theaters, the restaurants, the casino, the clubs, etcetera.

Other areas which may be noisy are around family suites, above or below the theater (sometimes noisy even during the day due to rehearsals), and below the galley (rolling carts and clanging dishes).

Also, you could hear clanging around any service area where the stewards are. The service areas are easy to spot in the long hallways of the cabin areas.

Cabins located on lower levels and towards the back of the ship sometimes experience engine noise or vibrations such as the lowering and raising of the anchor.

If you are on one of the lower levels in a cabin with a window, you may not like the sound of splashing waves hitting on the window. Something else to consider.

You'll hear of people who find this sound relaxing while others find it entirely annoying.

Chapter 1 - PLANNING YOUR CRUISE

As you prepare to book your cabin on-line, look at the deck plan of the ship and be sure others cannot see into your cabin from their balcony. This is rare, but occasionally occurs.

Oftentimes, ships are built with tiered cabins, so you may be able to see below into someone else's balcony (not the cabin). You may want to ask about this when you book your room.

Commit your cabin number to memory. It is awkward to be walking the long halls looking at doors that all look alike trying to find your room.

And while you are looking at the deck plan searching for a cabin, see where adjoining rooms are and avoid those, if possible. Cruisers with adjoining rooms are usually families with kids or someone having a cruise celebration party (during the whole cruise).

If you are traveling with children, you may want to book a cabin near the ship's children's area.

The previously mentioned app, Ship Mate, will provide your ship's deck plan. Or the cruise line's website will also have a deck plan. Ship Mate has lots of information on it, but please read their terms of service carefully.

Cruise Control

The furniture in staterooms is super heavy. This is because of possible rough seas. Get used to the way it is arranged because you may not be able to move it.

I have seen some people bring those edge protectors on their trip to avoid bumps and bruises from furniture. I don't find this necessary unless there are small kiddos.

As mentioned earlier, if you require a handicap accessible cabin, you may need to book it early as these go quickly. There is ordinarily no additional charge for these cabins.

The cruise lines will make sure the people who book these cabins are, in fact, handicapped.

If they find someone is not handicapped or even less handicapped than another guest may be, the front desk may move the less handicapped guests to another room. They reserve these rooms for the guests who need them.

All cabins have safes for your valuables. You simply choose your own code and program it on the safe.

I have forgotten and left items out which seemingly should have been in the safe, but we have

Chapter 1 - PLANNING YOUR CRUISE

been on lots of cruises and have never had an issue with theft.

Be careful you do not leave something in the safe when you leave to go home from your trip. Check every nook and cranny inside the safe.

If the mattress on your bed is too soft or too hard, the staff will provide you with whatever is needed to get the mattress to your liking, even bringing a different mattress to you. All you have to do is ask.

We have never had a problem with a bed being uncomfortable on any ship we've ever cruised on.

You will have a small refrigerator in your cabin. The items in there are not free. In fact, they can be costly. If you are not interested in the contents, have your cabin steward empty the fridge so you can store your own water, Cokes, or other items in it.

Storage in cabins is limited. However, you will find storage places in areas you least expect it.

Check the stool you are sitting on. It may open with storage underneath it. Pull on mirrors by the vanity (not too hard though, please). They likely open to a nice long set of small shelves for storage.

Cruise Control

Take a peek under the sofa. You may find storage there as well. I utilize windowsills to set items on.

If you have a special celebration occurring while you are on board, it is fun to decorate your cabin door. Or perhaps a holiday like Christmas is occurring while you cruise. Hang an inexpensive wreath on your door.

How about hearts all over your door for Valentine's Day? Have fun with your door!

Cruisers enjoy walking the long hallway glancing at the cute decorations. Always puts me in a celebratory mood. I've even seen couples traveling with other couples have contests for who has the best cabin door deco. Always fun!

Look at craft stores for scrapbooking decorations specific to cruising. You could make decorations relevant to your ports of call.

I've seen people decorate their door with items from their state. Also, big banners saying what they are celebrating. Birthdays, anniversaries, etcetera.

If you decorate your door, you will have no problem finding it among all the hundreds of other doors in the long hallway where every door looks exactly like your door.

Chapter 1 - PLANNING YOUR CRUISE

I have seen selfies on doors too. You may see other people taping their selfies to YOUR door! Lots of fun!

Most everything in your cabin is magnetic. You can purchase magnets in any form, including rolls. Simply cut the magnet the size you need.

If you did not bring enough magnets, attach a string on the inside of your door and suspend it over the door (to the outside facing the hallway). Tape items such as postcards to the string.

It is frowned upon to use tape on the walls or doors of your cabin. You do not want to scratch the wall or pull off some of the paint with the tape.

The stewards do not like the icky adhesive tape leaves because they are the ones to clean it up. Too time-consuming for them! Don't blame them, though, as they are always in a hurry to get things ready for the next guests coming on board for the next cruise.

We have seen cruisers use painter's tape. It does not have a stickiness to it, yet it holds.

If you have little ones crawling or walking around your cabin, painter's tape works great for taping cords and items to keep their little fingers away.

Cruise Control

Use your imagination. Have fun with your cabin door. It adds to yours and everyone else's vacation enjoyment.

I have never seen or heard of any type of theft of door decorations, but I would not put anything of value on the door.

We have been cruising for about 28 years, and I must say, the rest rooms in the cabins have improved tremendously in this time frame. You *can* make the most of them!

They used to be tiny and cramped. Today, they are more luxurious and accommodating. Most are still small, but if you pack right, you will find ways to organize and use the space wisely.

There are no vents in the cabin bathrooms, so consider bringing some type of sachets or some other form of room deodorizer.

You will have a shower and the space is cramped. Watch your head if you bend forward.

You may want to keep your showers short since there is no ventilation for steam and humidity. Most, if not all, have a removable shower head with a spray hose attached.

Chapter 1 - PLANNING YOUR CRUISE

In the balcony and suite cabins, the bathrooms are much larger. Some have tubs.

You will have a blow dryer in your cabin vanity, not in the bathroom. It will be attached inside the drawer, so you will not be able to move it except the length of the cord on it.

Be aware the toilets in these cabins flush differently than what you are used to. They are comparable to airplane toilets where you hear the loud swooshing sound when it is flushed.

Again, the swooshing sound in the toilets is loud in your cabin, so do not be alarmed. It is functioning the way it is made to function, loud!

Plugs are limited in cabins and cabin bathrooms. Bring an adapter. We have been on ships where surge protectors are not allowed. Leave it home if you're not sure about your ship's policy on this.

A way to keep from disturbing others in your cabin is to bring along some of those glow sticks for nighttime bathroom trips.

An interesting thing which people may notice, especially if this is your first cruise, trash cans are not plentiful on the ship. You will have one, possibly two, in your cabin.

Cruise ships do not like trash cans or bins sitting around, so they are limited. If you leave your trash on a table, on a chair or wherever you leave it, it will not be there long because a staff member will quickly pick it up.

K. CRUISE TERMINOLOGY

Wherever your vacation takes you, before you go, attempt to learn important terms and phrases in the language of your destinations.

Purchase a phrase book of the language for the country you're going to. These come in handy. Learn how to say hello, goodbye, please, and thank you.

No matter where your destination is, there is one *universal* gesture the whole world knows, a *smile*. Use it often! Especially on your ship! There will be friendly people everywhere.

Following are terms you may hear while preparing for your cruise and while onboard your ship. You will meet crew members from all over the world on your ship, but most often, the common language they will speak is English.

We have never had an issue communicating with a crew member.

Chapter 1 - PLANNING YOUR CRUISE

Aft – The stern or back of the ship.

Assigned seating – Fixed-time dining for cruisers in the main dining room; you will sit at the same table with the same people every night if you choose assigned seating. This is a great way to get to know your fellow cruisers sitting at your table. You can ask for another table if you are not comfortable.

Atrium – This is the central area on the ship, four or five, sometimes more, decks high (open). This is where Guest Services is located as well as the excursion desk. This area is beautiful and is where a number of passengers choose to hang out. In the evenings you will see all types of entertainment in the atrium.

Balcony cabin – A cabin with a balcony a guest can sit outside on.

Beam – The widest part of a ship.

Berth – Where the ship is docked.

Bow – The front of the ship.

Bridge – The navigation room where the controls of the ship and helm (steering wheel) are located and where you will likely find the captain of the vessel.

Brig – This is the jail on ships, not all ships.

Cruise Control

Cruise Captain – The CEO (so to speak) of the ship, in charge of everything.

Cruise Director – The person in charge of most entertainment happening on the ship; shows, games, programs, etcetera. You will see the Cruise Director emcee the events.

Debark/debarkation – Among passengers, this term is interchangeable with disembark/disembarkation. Debark means when you leave the ship.

Deck – Any of the floors; deck 1, deck 2, deck 3, etcetera.

Deck plan – A map illustrating the staterooms and public area locations.

Duty-free – You will pay no tax on items purchased in duty-free shops on ships sailing in foreign waters.

Embark/embarkation – When you board the ship.

Excursion – This is the term for those booked fun trips you take when the ship is in port. There are a variety of excursions available.

First seating – The earliest seating in the main dining room.

Chapter 1 - PLANNING YOUR CRUISE

Forward – The direction towards the bow or front of the ship.

Galley – The main kitchen of the ship.

Gangway – The opening with a long plank where passengers board and exit the ship.

Helm – The steering wheel on the ship.

Infirmary – The ship's on-board clinic/medical facility.

Inside cabin – An interior cabin.

Knot – One knot is one nautical mile per hour, which is 1.15 miles per hour on land.

Lido – The part of the ship where the buffet is located and is on one of the top decks of the ship.

Midship – The middle of the ship.

Muster drill – The drill required by cruise lines for every passenger to attend in order to be briefed with safety procedures in case of emergency.

Oceanview cabin – A cabin with a window.

Open seating – Dining without any specific scheduled time.

Port of call – The ports you visit during your voyage.

Cruise Control

Port side – The left part of the ship as you face towards the front of the ship.

Promenade – Typically, the area on ships which house the shops, restaurants, carousels, etcetera.

Purser – Person responsible for onboard transactions, assisting guests with their individual needs such as lost and found, etcetera.

Reservation number – The reference number provided to you after you book a cruise.

Second seating – The latest seating in the main dining room.

Showroom – The main theater where shows, games, and other things of interest are held.

Stabilizer – Used for rough seas to keep the ship stable, this is something you hope they do not have to use.

Starboard – The right part of the ship as you face towards the front of the ship.

Stateroom or cabin – The term for your room/living quarters.

Stern – The back of the ship.

Suite – An upgraded cabin accommodation.

Chapter 1 - PLANNING YOUR CRUISE

Tender boat – The term for the small boats used to take passengers to and from the shore when the ship is anchored.

Veranda – Private balcony.

Wake – The visible wave on either side of a ship.

L. PORTS OF CALL & EXCURSIONS

First, a word of caution....at any port, you need to be on board at least 30 minutes before your ship is scheduled to set sail. You do not want to be one of those cruisers left in ports because they did not make it back in time for departure.

Depending on the circumstances of you getting stuck on land, the captain may or may not find a way for you to join the ship at the next port. If you're lucky, the next port may be home port.

As you start to book your excursions, keep in mind time is sometimes limited in ports. It is a smart idea to research and plan ahead what you may want to see in a certain port and your transportation to what you want to see.

On most cruise lines, you can book your shore excursions on-line far in advance of your cruise. Go to the cruise line's website, and you will find their extensive excursions listed, including the cost.

You may also book excursions on the cruise line's app.

It can get frustrating with long lines If you wait until you board the ship to head to the excursion desk to book your excursions.

If you received any type of onboard credit when you booked your cruise, it can customarily be applied toward an excursion you book on the ship.

You can also look on-line and book excursions through an independent tour company.

Doing your research ahead of time allows you to study the port cities and compare the excursions.

You may believe having only one day in port is not enough time to do what you want. If you research ahead of time, you can plan your schedule out. You may be surprised at what all you can do!

When booking through the cruise line, they may say there are limited spaces available for an excursion. They are trying to get you to sign up. We do not take this statement seriously.

Chapter 1 - PLANNING YOUR CRUISE

Oftentimes, people opt to grab an excursion right on the pier when they get off the ship. Most often, the excursions are less expensive on the pier.

Excursions are 40% to 60% (sometimes more) less if you book through a private tour company on-line or grab one on the pier from the tour guides. We have booked from tour companies and have never had a complaint.

However, they do not provide a guarantee you will be back on the ship at departure time. Booking through your cruise line provides this guarantee.

Honestly, we have never heard of anyone not making it back to the ship on time when they book their excursion on the pier.

Your travel guide from a private tour will be waiting on you at the pier, possibly holding a large sign with the name of their tour.

Always bring the company's phone number with you. And don't forget to tip them when your fun with them is over!

If you use a travel agent, they can book private tours for you and those in your group.

<u>Cruise Control</u>

The locals are more than willing to provide private tours for vacationers. These are normally inexpensive. What better way to learn the culture and see the highlights than with a local person, someone who lives there?

A number of excursions require an early arrival, and there will be tons of people trying to debark from the ship.

It may be wise to enjoy a beautiful day on the ship. Or you could have a relaxing breakfast in any number of the on-board restaurants and then debark after the rush is over.

Or you may want to forego getting off the ship at all if a particular port doesn't tickle your fancy. Think of the savings because you are eating your free meals on the ship for a port day!

There are cruisers who opt to take an afternoon excursion to avoid the early-morning rush of cruisers getting off the ship.

Depending on where your ports of call are, you may be required to board a tender if the waters are too shallow for the ship to pull next to the dock.

Chapter 1 - PLANNING YOUR CRUISE

A tender is a small boat, holding around 100 guests. These tenders travel back and forth from ship to shore every couple of minutes.

Keep in mind these tenders are customarily not wheelchair accessible. There are ships, however, that allow small wheelchairs on their tenders. It is a good idea to read the website of the cruise line you are traveling with to determine their policies with regard to persons with disabilities.

As the ship arrives in ports, after the ship has been cleared by local authorities, the captain or director will announce over the loudspeaker when it is okay to debark. Fun in the port begins!

By the way, don't try to take fruit off the ship. There are laws in most destinations not allowing this.

It is wise to make yourself familiar with the currencies where your ship will be making stops. Learn the important words in the language of the locals.

Grab a map of your location as soon as you get off the ship.

Whether you book your excursion through the ship or from another source, again, you will meet

Cruise Control

your excursion guide on the pier after you debark the ship.

There is an abundance of different types of excursions for each port. Do you want to relax on the beach? Shop? Tour the area? How about the zip line you've been wanting to try or grabbing a four-wheeler to ride?

One excursion we took on one of our cruises was an underwater scooter. What a blast!

You can swim with sharks or dolphins or stingrays, snorkel, go kayaking, party on a Catamaran, or go deep sea fishing. I've seen a scavenger hunt excursion where you go all over the town looking for clues.

The choices for excursions are endless.

There are all types of excursions. Horseback riding, coastal speedboat rides, scooters, or ATVs. You'll find about anything you can think of that's fun!

How about a glass-bottom boat? Those are always fun! You may even find a submarine to take an excursion on.

Chapter 1 - PLANNING YOUR CRUISE

There are city tours in most ports of call. We enjoy city tours to learn about the area we are visiting.

Cities often have double-decker buses. Always fun to relax on those and enjoy a scenic tour of the city. Oftentimes, you can hop on and hop off at your leisure, all for one price.

You will find deep sea fishing or fly-fishing in some ports. Scuba diving for the seasoned divers as well as beginning divers is available. If you are a certified scuba diver, do not forget your certification. They will not let you go diving without it.

Have you ever wanted to visit the Mayan Temples? You will undoubtedly find excursions available in various areas.

If flying through the air on a zip line or parasailing is on your bucket list, you will find it in most Caribbean ports. I've done it several times and would love to do it again.

You can rent jet skis. On the ones we've seen, you are required to stay in a line and with the group. Great for a beginner.

Cruise Control

You will see cruise passengers booking excursions together who do not even know each other. You may find savings if you book with a large group. In fact, you may get offered a free cabin!

You'll see cruisers who prefer to shop while on land. You will find a channel on your television which is strictly port and shopping information and shows on your television continuously.

You may find stores in ports are expensive, high-quality items. You may also find stores in ports which are much less expensive. There is an abundance of various shopping stores.

As much as it pains me to say this, thieves are everywhere. When you go ashore, reconsider before you wear a T-shirt or hat or carry a bag with your ship's logo on it. You could be a target of local thieves because they know you do not want to miss your ship.

It is tempting and easy to spend money in these ports, so you may want to take more cash than you plan to spend. The Caribbean ports take U.S. dollars, but not all ports all over the world do. You may want to research this before you leave.

Chapter 1 - PLANNING YOUR CRUISE

As previously mentioned, there is an app called XE Currency to assist you with converting different currencies from all over the world.

A wristwatch or a cell phone is an essential for off-the-ship excursions. No matter what port you are in, do not forget to keep your watch or phone on the ship's time.

Don't change your watch. If you miss the ship, they will not wait. If the ship's time to leave the port is at 6:00, it will leave at 6:00. Not 6:15 or 6:05.

We always return to the ship at least one hour before departure.

If you happen to get left in the port, it will be your own responsibility to get to the next port or home. If you get left, you may not have your passport with you which will make things even more complicated.

One caveat to the previous paragraph. It is our understanding, though we have never tested this, if you book your shore excursion through the ship, the ship provides a guarantee it will not leave you. Or if you do get left, the cruise line will fly you to the next port.

The ships pay for the time they are docked in ports, so it may be less expensive for them to fly you to the next port instead of sitting there docked, waiting on passengers.

There are cruisers who do not take shore excursions. They prefer to browse the shops, eat, relax, get some sun on the beach.

If you do go to the beach, be sure to keep ALL of your belongings with you. No one likes to imagine a thief, but you never know.

If you prefer not to take an excursion, grab a taxi and head to the town. Oftentimes, the locals can guide you to better places to visit at their port. Ask them. They are more often than not willing to lend a hand to you.

May I suggest if you do grab a taxi, please agree on your price with the driver before you get into the taxi. We have heard (not experienced) taxi drivers charging way too much.

Oftentimes, we take a taxi with others from the ship, as this saves expense. Or you can take public transportation such as a bus or scooter.

The option to rent a car in ports is there as well. Personally, I do not like to rent cars because I am on vacation to relax, not to have to worry about driving on the wrong side of the road or getting into a

Chapter 1 - PLANNING YOUR CRUISE

situation, (such as an accident), preventing me from making it back to the ship.

If you do opt to rent a car, try getting a group of people together to rent it. Like with cabs, it is, of course, much less expensive this way.

Bear in mind you must have cash or a credit card to shop in the local stores on land. Your cruise card will not work. Yep, we've seen people try to use their cruise card on land. Strange, huh?

You may never be at this particular place again. Gain as much knowledge as you can about the area and the culture of the people.

If you are looking to shop in port, walk further away from the debarkation area. You will see much better prices. Oftentimes, the shops right there where the ship docks are owned by the ships. Prices may be higher.

Keep in mind, oftentimes stores and shops in port will be closed on Sundays. Some restaurants may be closed on Mondays.

You are allowed to get on and off the ship as often as you'd like while docked at one of the ports. Hop back on the ship for lunch. Then hop back off to do more shopping.

Some cruisers will plan an excursion at the home port city for the day the ship returns home. Why not, if your flight is not until the next day?

Remember, you are able to book your excursions on-line before you ever leave home. Sometimes excursions sell out. Book ahead if you can!

M. PASSPORTS & PRE-CRUISE DOCUMENTS

Depending on your destination, you will likely need a passport for your cruise. You should apply for one as soon as you have decided on your trip.

The customary time to receive a passport is four to six weeks. However, you can pay an expedite fee to receive it quicker.

You may get rejected for some reason, so you want to apply way ahead of your trip.

You can obtain a passport at most post offices. Or you can apply on-line at www.travel.state.gov.

Every person traveling internationally is required to have a passport. You will need one to get back into the United States.

Check with the State Department for entry requirements for where you are traveling to and

Chapter 1 - PLANNING YOUR CRUISE

from. A passport is in force for 10 years from date of issue.

If you are traveling internationally, your passport cannot expire for six months after the last day of your cruise. It must be an original passport. They will not accept a copy!

If you are traveling with friends or family, be sure to ask them about their passport. We have been on cruises before where part of a cruiser's family had to stay home because they did not know they needed to apply for one far in advance.

When booking your cruise, whether on-line or through a travel agent, you will receive a Passenger Immigration Form (PIF). This is a required form when traveling internationally and must be filled out in its entirety. It is self-explanatory.

You will receive your boarding pass only after you have completed the required documents. Required documents include (and may not be limited to) your Passenger Immigration Form, your emergency contact information, your Health Declaration Form, and establishing your on-board account with a credit card.

Cruise Control

The Health Declaration Form is customarily handed to you right before check-in at the port. It asks if you are or have been sick. Do people honestly say yes to this question? Yes, they sure do. Does not mean you won't be able to board.

It is probable if someone lied on the document and it could be proven they lied (which it likely can be), they could be sued. I would be honest on this health form no matter what.

If you book your cruise on-line or choose to use a travel agent, you will receive all documentation necessary for you to take your cruise.

You will need to have all your documents in order and be ready to set sail on your departure date. It is my understanding you are able to pre-register on-line with all cruise lines. We have always pre-registered with no problems.

Make your cruise companion(s) aware you must have *all* of your documents prepared and ready to go on the day of embarkation.

It is a great idea to make two or three copies of all your important documents. Passport, driver's license, airline tickets, credit cards, and any other important documents.

Chapter 1 - PLANNING YOUR CRUISE

Leave a copy of this information at home, and leave a copy in the safe in your cabin. It is wise to take a copy of your passport on shore in ports and leave the real thing in your safe.

At the end of your cruise, you will be required to fill out a U.S. Customs Declaration Form if you have traveled to a different country. Your cabin steward will leave the form in your cabin the night before arriving to home port.

You are supposed to list on this form every item you purchased while abroad. However, most often people will categorize items, such as souvenirs, jewelry, etc. They may ask you to itemize them. We have never been asked.

The purpose of the Customs Declaration is, of course, for you to declare what you purchased. As of this writing, each person is allowed $800 in merchandise per person before an import tax may be applied.

Keep your receipts handy upon arriving to customs. They may ask to see them. Keep in mind, the name you made your cruise reservation in *must* match the name on your passport. All your paperwork for the cruise must match your personal identification.

Your name on your passport must be the exact name on the ship's manifest.

In other words, if you get married between the time you book your cruise and the date of your cruise, you must still use the name on your passport to book the cruise (if you have not had time to get a new passport with your new name).

If you are on your honeymoon, you will need to be sure your passport has your married name on it. Again, the name on your passport must match the name the cruise is booked under, whether it be maiden name or married name.

If you are a frequent traveler who receives countless immigration stamps in your passport, you may want to double check it to be sure you have enough blank pages in it for your vacation travel.

N. SAVE MONEY WHEN BOOKING YOUR CRUISE

If you do your research, you will see it is possible to save money when booking your cruise. There are constant deals being advertised on a daily basis.

The closer you get to your sail date, the more the ship wants to fill its cabins. They sometimes offer booked passengers a discounted upgrade.

Chapter 1 - PLANNING YOUR CRUISE

Oftentimes, this offer is on a bidding system. Of course, the higher your bid, the greater the chance of receiving an upgrade.

You may get a resident discount, depending upon where you reside. Ports within driving distance are trying to fill those ships.

You are eligible for a past-cruise discount through their loyalty program. The ships we've been on have all had a loyalty program.

They sometimes refer to this as a loyalty discount. They want to reward passengers who stick with them. Often you will receive dinners, beverage packages, upgrades and other perks as well.

If you can be flexible and sail at the last minute, you may be able to book a cruise for upwards of 80% less.

Last minute is anywhere from two or three days before sail date to 90 days out from sail date. If you can leave on the spur of the moment, you could find a rock-bottom cruise price!

Sometimes travel agents have perks such as paid gratuities and free upgrades they can offer, but you will need to ask them. They may not volunteer, so come right out and ask them, "Do you have any perks or bonuses you can throw in?"

There are cruise lines which allow children under a certain age to vacation for free or at a huge discounted price. Most cruise lines do not allow babies under six months old to cruise. However, check with the cruise line.

If you do take a baby on your trip, I strongly advise bringing all of your own needed items for your baby. Some ships do provide diapers (at a great cost).

If your little one is used to having their own potty seat, they may not want to use the big toilet seat in the cabin. Think of some unique way to turn it into a smaller seat.

I've seen portable folding tiny seats for the little ones on Amazon. They fit right on top of the big toilets.

There are parents who will inevitably complain their tiny ones cannot go into any of the on-board pools. No matter what you say, they have a difficult time understanding fellow cruisers do not want to swim with pee and boo-boo.

Chapter 1 - PLANNING YOUR CRUISE

If you use a travel agent to book your cruise, you may find better deals, especially if you use a travel agent who specializes in cruises. They will also keep your booking up to date should a discounted price come up.

If you are using a travel agent, keep in mind this cruise vacation can be tailored to exactly what *you* want. They will be super informed about your cruise ship as well as the cost.

They can sometimes alert you to price drops and customarily have the ability to get the lower rate for you.

You may be able to have your gratuities pre-paid by the cruise line. Ask your travel agent about this as it could be great savings!

And don't forget to ask for onboard credits. They are plentiful, but sometimes you need to ask about them. On-board credits may be offered to entice you to book with a certain company or person.

Remember, on-board credits are per cabin, not per person (unless otherwise specified).

You will need to use these credits while you are on the ship. They are nontransferable. You can use the credits while on board for anything you pay for.

Cruise Control

When you book your cruise, whether yourself or through a travel agent, you may be offered perks to entice you to book. Be sure to check the difference in the cost of the exact same cruise, with perks and without perks.

Look for ports within driving distance of your home to save money. Galveston, Seattle, California, New Orleans, Florida and many more.

Also, you do not want to book an early flight home on debarkation day. You are taking a chance of missing your flight if you do.

We have found things run smoothly on the morning of debarkation, but you never know what might happen. Unforeseen circumstances sometimes happen.

If you are able to drive to your destination port, parking is plentiful at the terminal and convenient as well. It may be more expensive than parking lots away from the terminal. Oftentimes, your hotel will offer parking at a reasonable rate.

Call the terminal for parking costs before you leave if you are driving to your ship's departure terminal.

Chapter 1 - PLANNING YOUR CRUISE

There could be thousands of cars parked at the pier, so if you do park there, take several pictures of the area where your car is parked. When you return, you will have no problem locating it.

I've met folks who believe booking a cruise at the last minute is less expensive. Ships are trying to fill their cabins. Other folks say it is less expensive to book your cruise six to nine months in advance.

We have never been able to figure out either theory as we have received some excellent discounts both ways.

You may find excellent incentives given by the ships to get you to book early.

If you book a future cruise on the current cruise you are taking (there is a desk specifically for you to do that), you may be offered reduced deposits or no deposits, free onboard credit, even reduced airfare sometimes.

We have found cruise prices vary from week to week. However, if you pay attention to the final date for cancellation on a certain cruise you may be looking at, try booking your cruise around this time frame.

Cruise Control

There will be cancellations, and the ship will want to fill those cancelled rooms (and at a great rate).

If a ship changes its itinerary, this sometimes causes the prices to drop. People cancel their cruise (100% refund) if there is a change in their cruise itinerary that they are not happy with, so the ships are trying to fill those empty cabins at great discounts.

If your itinerary changes before you set sail, the cruise line will often offer you the option of changing your cruise, if you prefer.

You will likely be expected to put a deposit on your cruise, especially if you book far in advance. The deposits required are not large, $50 or $100 per person.

These deposits are customarily non-refundable. Sometimes they will refund a prorated amount.

Cruises during hurricane season are less costly. This is the less busy time for ships. Possibly great savings for the guests.

Keep in mind, your itinerary may change mid-trip as ships will navigate around storms. If your itinerary does need to change, you likely will not be disappointed in the new destination.

Chapter 1 - PLANNING YOUR CRUISE

You probably know people are afraid of cruising simply because of the possibility of hurricanes or tropical storms. These ships cost billions of dollars to build and have thousands of lives on board.

I am confident in saying no ship captain is going to cruise towards a hurricane. They will go around it. It may sometimes be on the outskirts of a storm, but they will cruise around the storms as much as possible.

You may see weather in the far distance putting a frown on your face, but your ship will sail around it as much as possible.

Couple more points about saving.

Most cruise lines offer discounts for certain travelers. Senior citizens, active and retired military personnel, EMTs, firefighters and police personnel, teachers.

Past-guest discounts are also offered on most cruise lines.

As of the time of this writing, AARP offers members a five percent discount on cruises booked at least nine months in advance.

Oftentimes, certain states also offer special pricing.

People believe if you stick with one cruise line you will get extra perks and benefits. We have not found this to be particularly true.

However, it could be beneficial to become a member if the cruise line has a membership program as you may get a previous guest discount.

O. TRAVEL INSURANCE

Sometimes, we spend months planning for our dream vacation. Then, out of the blue, our throat begins to hurt, our nose begins to drip, we are exhausted and achy.

We all know stress is a breeding ground for getting sick. Yet in preparation for your trip, stress seems to take over. It's a fact, planning for a vacation can be truly stressful, especially on our bodies.

In fact, beginning the trip is stressful as well. New place to sleep, people all over the place you do not know, no organized routine you are accustomed to.

When you commence planning your trip is the time to initiate extra precautions for your health.

Chapter 1 - PLANNING YOUR CRUISE

You don't want to ruin your dream vacation getting ill while traveling.

There will be a medical facility with a full medical staff on board your ship. This area is designed to handle any emergency. However, in the unlikely event of major issues, such as strokes or heart attacks, the passenger could be airlifted to the nearest medical facility.

Please be patient if this happens. Medical issues are outside of anyone's control. The health of the sick person is what matters at this point.

If they need to be airlifted to proper care, your cruise fun will resume once the emergency has been taken care of.

Be grateful it is not you or one of your loved ones, and have an extra dose of patience during this awful time for the seriously ill person and their family.

If there is an emergency at home while you are cruising, the Guest Services' team will accommodate you in whatever way they can. They are there to help.

There are cruisers who will purchase travel insurance before their cruise. We have been on ships where fellow passengers became ill or had an accident, and their health insurance would not cover them because they were out of the country.

You may want to research this, as a number of insurance companies do not cover out-of-country claims.

Some travelers prefer to purchase travel insurance simply because of the peace of mind it brings, especially for worry-warts.

These policies may not cover pre-existing conditions. Read these documents thoroughly, especially the fine print, before you purchase.

There could be delays and possibly cancellations, sickness or any other number of unforeseen situations your travel insurance will cover if you purchase it.

If you do purchase travel insurance, be sure to take all your documents with you on your trip.

P. WHERE DO CREW MEMBERS/STAFF MEMBERS LIVE?

There are *crew* members. Then there are *staff* members.

Chapter 1 - PLANNING YOUR CRUISE

Crew members are the ones who interact less with guests, such as waiters and busboys, housekeeping, maintenance.

Staff members interact with the guests frequently. These include the captain and his/her team, guest relations, videographers, the entertainment staff.

All the way in the bottom of the ship, (usually on decks 2 and 3), is where the crew members live.

From what we've heard, it is not boring on the staff floors at all. They have their own gym, library, bars, game room, restaurants, and other places the guests have upstairs.

Interestingly, most of the workers on ships get hours off, not full days and rarely get weekends off. I can imagine plenty of power naps going on among them!

Did you know the tips added to your bill at the end of your cruise are divided among a large number of employees? Remember this when you tip. They are deserving of every cent they receive.

These tips are generally divided among the waiters, assistant waiters, and headwaiters as well as the housekeeping staff, including cabin attendants. Some ships include Guest Services in these tips.

Every ship does this differently, but the above explanation is what we have experienced on the ships we've been on.

Chapter 2 - PACKING TIPS & HINTS

A. DON'T FORGET THESE

(some essentials and maybe not-so-essentials but great to have)

If you have an inside cabin, you will want to bring a nightlight of some sort.

I always take a nightlight regardless of what type of cabin we are staying in because I find it useful for a number of different things. Looking for something I dropped on the floor, finding an earring, reading at night, etcetera.

If you are traveling with children, they may be used to having a nightlight.

Small alarm clocks come in handy if you do not want to rely on your cell phone. The ship will have wake-up calls available as well, but some people do not like to rely on others to wake them.

If you miss your excursion from oversleeping, the excursion staff may not wait for you. And you may not have cell service in all the places your ship goes, so a wake-up call is important.

Cruisers bring extension cords as the cabin may have a lack of electrical outlets. We take an electric

Cruise Control

converter because we have been on ships where there were no 110 outlets.

A power strip, (non-surge to make the cruise line happy with it), with a USB port will come in handy if you need to use your computer or charge something.

More and more ships are not allowing power strips of any kind. So, stick with a small extension cord.

You can buy small, portable USB chargers as well.

Keep in mind, countries across the world could have different power outlets than what you may be accustomed to. Check this before your trip, and make sure to purchase adapters or converters if you need them.

Not sure I have ever had the need for this, but I take a small flashlight. It makes me more secure in the event of a power outage. We have never been on a ship during a power outage, but you never know.

Take along a small roll of duct tape. You would be surprised at what you can use it for (just not the doors or walls).

Chapter 2 - PACKING TIPS & HINTS

If noise bothers you, you may need to bring along earplugs. You will find there are quiet places on ships as well as extremely noisy places.

I have seen people toting around noise-canceling headphones. But there are notably quiet places on the ships as well, including the adults only Solarium.

Depending on your destination(s), you may spend a lot of time in the sun, so do not forget your sunscreen. You will need it!

You may believe you never burn, but it is all but certain you will burn on a cruise, unless you are going to a destination with little sun.

The sun is sometimes much different when you are on the open seas. You do not want to get sunburned on your first day. It could make the rest of your trip miserable!

Monitor your stay in the sun closely. Aloe can be soothing for sunburn.

Bring a wide-brimmed hat if you burn easily to protect your face and possibly neck from the sun. Put on sunscreen anyway. If you do not like to wear hats, try a visor.

Cruise Control

We have never used one but have seen other cruisers use a sunscreen stick. Takes the stickiness and mess out of using a liquid sunscreen.

You may consider purchasing a pair or two of sunglasses with SUV protection. Bring along an extra pair. This is one of the most lost items on ships.

The ship may visit ports with rocky terrain. Sometimes sharp objects can be hidden in the sand. Don't forget to bring water shoes. If you tear your feet up, the rest of your trip will possibly be miserable.

My feet have a tendency to swell when I travel, so I always take along a pair of flip-flops to wear until the swelling subsides by the second or third day.

I always take wrinkle spray when we cruise. Put it in a small spray bottle. Or you can purchase a travel size bottle. Works well to remove wrinkles in clothes which have been bundled in a suitcase.

Turn on the hot water in your shower, let it run and steam the bathroom. Hang your wrinkled article in there, and you may see the wrinkles disappear!

You can purchase wrinkle release products as well. We take along a small bottle of Downy Wrinkle Release.

Chapter 2 - PACKING TIPS & HINTS

The ships do have laundry services, but they can sometimes be costly. There are actual laundry rooms as well. Ask your steward or at the Guest Services' desk.

A positive way to look at doing laundry is if you pack less clothes and wash them by hand or in the ship's laundry, your baggage fees through the airline will be much less.

We pack half of each of our belongings in two (or more) different suitcases. If a piece of luggage gets lost or misplaced, we still have one suitcase with at least some belongings for both of us.

Can't bring electrical appliances on board. Do not bring an iron of any kind. They are not allowed on ships. Steamers are allowed on some ships, not all.

On most ships we've been on, you simply have to request an iron and they are happy to bring you one.

Don't forget plastic trash bag(s) to put your dirty clothes in, unless you love to do laundry while cruising.

Some type of hamper or bag will work for dirty clothes, but I use a plain trash bag because it takes no room to pack. When you leave for home from your cruise, you're putting the same clothes in the suitcase. Use the bag to separate the clean clothes from the dirty clothes.

If you love to do laundry, you will need to take your own laundry detergent. I put a small amount in a Ziploc baggie or take a pod or two in case I need to handwash something.

Pre-wash wipes are ideal for getting out spots or stains.

Candles are also not allowed on ships. However, we've seen folks bring those battery-operated LED candles. If you're looking for ambiance in your cabin, these are ideal. Some of these LED candles even have remote controls.

It is important to remember these LED candles will look like a flame from far away. If someone from one of those tiered balconies you see on some ships sees the flicker through your balcony door and thinks it's real, you may find security rushing to put it out. Not kidding. We've seen this happen!

Lighters are not allowed on ships.

Don't forget to take your wristwatch. There are no clocks in the cabins. And clocks on the ship are limited.

Chapter 2 - PACKING TIPS & HINTS

On port days, you will need a watch or clock of some type, especially if you choose to leave your cell phone in your cabin safe

Again (because this is so important), do not change the time on your watch/cell. Keep it on ship's time no matter what time it is in the port.

Bring plenty of cash. The ATM machines on ships charge from $5 to $8 per transaction.

If you must get cash, go to the casino and insert your cruise card into a slot machine.

Choose the amount you want to put on your cruise card, don't play the slot machine, cash out and take the cash-out ticket to the cashier. They will pay you in cash.

This is an inventive way to avoid those high ATM fees. Remember, the amount you choose will be put on your cruise card which will be on your bill the last day of your cruise.

I would not make a habit of this, however, as your ability to add cash may be frozen if you are doing this too frequently. Get all the cash you need at one time.

Cruise Control

This also works if you have on-board credits you will not be using. Cash it out in the casino.

Keep in mind casinos are only allowed to operate in international waters. They will be closed while in ports.

Are you one of those people who cannot sleep unless a fan is blowing? If this is you, bring one of those tiny fans to sit right next to your head on the nightstand.

A white noise machine works well too. An app called White Noise Lite is ideal If you do not sleep well in total silence.

You might want to take along a card the size of a credit card or maybe a card from a deck of cards for the slot by the cabin door for your lights. You normally would use your cabin key for this.

People sometimes forget their key and leave it in the slot by their door. And you need your key (which is your cruise card) to make purchases all over the ship!

On one cruise we were on, it was not necessary to put a card in the slot for the electric in the cabin.

Chapter 2 - PACKING TIPS & HINTS

One of the most important items to take on a cruise is your swimsuit! You may be spending tons of time at the pool or the beach.

You are allowed to walk to most places on the ship with your swimsuit on, but I recommend a cover-up (to be considerate of others).

Most people know what clothes they need to pack, but honestly, you'd be surprised what we have seen people forget. Underwear, pajamas, dress shoes for formal night, a belt, swimsuit cover-up, among other things.

You might want to take a notepad or some type of paper for making notes on. Trust me, when you get back home and look at your pictures, you will not remember where you were and what cruise day you were there.

Another option we learned from a fellow cruiser for remembering when you are at which port is to take a photo early in the morning of the floor in front of the elevator where the day of the week is always displayed.

You will be able to tell from the picture preceding that day's photos where you were and on what day.

Cruise Control

I take along an extra pair of reading glasses as well as an extra contact lens. It is not uncommon for people to misplace or lose both of these items.

When you are in certain ports, it is important to have mosquito or insect repellant. If you do not want to pack it, it is for sale at most shops. We have never needed to use insect repellant on the ships we've been on.

If you are prone to rashes, don't forget to take some type of rash guard.

If you tend to experience motion sickness, bring something to alleviate that. Some people bring over-the-counter Dramamine or wear a Scopolamine patch right under their ear. These are over-the-counter patches.

Others wear some type of bracelet, brand name of ReliefBand or SeaBand, they swear helps them with the swaying of the ship. These bracelets apply acupuncture to the inside of the wrist which is supposed to stop the nausea.

Others swear by using ginger to alleviate sea sickness.

Try going outside. A cool breeze works great for seasickness, as does fresh air!

Chapter 2 - PACKING TIPS & HINTS

Guest Services will customarily keep samples of seasickness pills on hand for cruisers.

We've only been in one storm causing a tiny bit of swaying. Honestly, ships these days are extremely stable, rarely swaying. They have state-of-the-art stabilizers keeping the swaying of the ship at bay.

You can bring reusable water bottles from home. This will save you a ton of money. Simply refill it in your cabin or a water fountain. This is perfectly acceptable with the cruise lines. Spending so much time in the sun, you will be thirsty.

If you are an avid coffee drinker, pack your own coffee mug. The cups on board are often small. Simply fill your own coffee mug and head off to enjoy your day.

I can say we have never had a problem using our charge cards in any port, but we have heard of people who have had issues with this.

Bring cash to the ports in case you run into this problem somewhere. You would hate to find something you want, a souvenir for a loved one, you are unable to purchase because you have no cash.

The street markets and vendors who sell souvenirs would prefer cash.

Cruise Control

Before you bring any item or souvenir back home into your respective country, it is wise to check online for items you may not be allowed to bring into your country.

As an example, items such as ivory, feathers, and straw are prohibited in some countries.

When you are purchasing souvenirs, consider the weight. I've seen people who will ship the item to their home from a port on their trip in order to save overweight luggage fees at the airport.

More on don't forget items….

Take extra safety pins. You do not want to fall overboard grabbing for a towel as the wind blows it off the chair on your balcony! Pin it together.

You may lose a button off your blouse or rip something. You'll be glad you have those pins.

We've seen people bring small rolls of duct tape or double-sided tape for emergencies like taping a hem. I pack a tiny sewing kit with the essentials in it.

Pack waterproof Band-Aids. If you get a scratch or bite or blisters, you won't spend time waiting for the cabin steward to go find you one.

Chapter 2 - PACKING TIPS & HINTS

Same with nail clippers. Sure, they can find you some clippers, but why wait? Take a small pair.

Ladies, do not forget your nail glue. It is likely a guarantee you will break a nail in all the fun. Super glue works well, too, and you can use it for other things as well.

Bring aspirin, Ibuprofen, Motrin, Benadryl, Imodium, or whatever you choose to help alleviate pain or other ailments. Just put a few of each in a small container.

Sometimes too much sun (among other things on cruise ships) can cause headaches. Or you may find you have sore muscles from walking all day. They sell these types of medications on board, but they can be pricey.

We've seen other cruisers bring a small dental kit due to issues they were having with their teeth before they left home. This is something to consider if you're having dental problems.

While there are doctors and nurses on board, there are no dentists on board.

I put various items in Ziploc baggies. Tums, throat lozenges, anti-itch cream, allergy meds, eyedrops, and items such as that.

<u>Cruise Control</u>

Take a bunch of different-sized Ziploc baggies. They come in handy for tons of stuff. Wet clothes, cell phone on the beach, camera on the beach. I put all our small items in baggies.

I put my make-up and make-up brushes in baggies to keep from having to rummage through other items looking for the brushes. (I am always in a hurry to get out of the cabin and on to having fun.)

I find the Ziplocs come in handy for a number of things.

You can purchase a waterproof phone case for your cell phone for easy access to it. I've seen them on Amazon for around $8-$10.

A pair of binoculars is always nice to have on excursions. We do not take binoculars, simply because we do not want to lug them around.

Ever thought of walkie-talkies for your cruise? These are especially handy if you have small children or elderly folks cruising with you. You will want to keep these set to a low volume to keep from disturbing fellow passengers.

Don't forget your essentials like shaving cream, razors, makeup remover, moisturizers, lotions, shampoo, and conditioner for your hair.

Chapter 2 - PACKING TIPS & HINTS

They supply shampoo, but some ships do not supply conditioner. They supply bar soap as well, but I oftentimes take a small bar of my own that is more fragrant than theirs.

Waterproof mascara also comes in handy. In all likelihood, you will spend time in the pools, ocean and sun. You do not want running mascara, right?

I always take a lint roller as well. Cannot tell you how frequently this has come in handy after clothes have been jammed into suitcases! They sell small lint rollers at most grocery stores.

Take a small can of Static Guard for those clingy items.

Along with my toothbrush and toothpaste, I take along some dental floss. It has come in handy for more things than my teeth!

Bring some air freshener (you'll be glad you did). Or take some of those car air fresheners, hang them around your room.

I hang Scentsy Paks as well as Scentsy Car Bars, and our cabin always smells wonderful.

You may get a bathroom with a shower curtain. An inventive idea is to take along some clothes pins or binder clips to attach to the bottom of the shower curtain to keep it from blowing out. The weight of the clothes pins will keep it hanging straight.

Clothes pins or binder clips require little space in your luggage. Store them inside your packed shoes. They are also excellent to use for your towel out by the pool. If it's a windy day, clamp your towel onto your chair.

I am always amazed at how handy those binder clips are! I use one to keep our paperwork together while cruising.

It goes without saying (but I'll say it anyway), you *will* need comfortable walking shoes on a cruise. I learned this the hard way. People, especially women, want to look cute and in style. But let me tell you, your feet will thank you for it if you take comfortable shoes.

There is sometimes rainy weather, depending on your destination, so don't forget your umbrella. Mine folds small. But it does the job. When you get off the ship in a port where the weather looks iffy, don't forget to take it!

Same thing with a raincoat. You can buy one at the dollar store that will fold to a tiny square. Grab

Chapter 2 - PACKING TIPS & HINTS

one, and if you run into rain, you'll be glad you did. A large plastic trash bag from home makes an excellent cover too.

You can find the average temperatures for most cruise ports at www.weather.com.

Another tip I found from several frequent cruisers is to take one of those shoe storage hangers, the kind you hang on the door. You can put all kinds of items in them! Plus, it keeps things organized.

Bathrooms are generally not big on ships (unless you are in a suite). These shoe organizers come in handy for hairbrushes, combs, shaving cream, razors, and tons of other bath items. And the shoe organizer takes little room in your luggage.

I am a clean freak, so I take disinfecting handwipes everywhere I go. Your cabin will, of course, be kept immaculate, but I always wipe everything in our cabin with a towelette anyway, first thing. Remote control, phone, toilet seat and handle, sink handles, lamp buttons, anything we touch.

It's simply another precaution. I do this anytime we are out of town anywhere.

Cruise Control

Common sense tells us there are plenty of germs on board. Take special care while eating, especially in the buffet, to frequently wash your hands. Hand sterilizer is provided on a stand before you enter restaurants. You simply hold your hand under it, and the sterilizer squirts out. It is motion activated.

Hand sanitizer is available all over the ship. Take some handwipes with you anyway for extra precaution.

Lanyards are those strings you attach cruise cards to and hang around your neck or attach to a loop on your clothes.

If you do not have a lanyard, Guest Services or the casino will provide one to you at no charge. They will punch a hole in your card for you if you ask.

Hundreds of people lose their cruise cards on every cruise. If you lose yours, then you will need to go to the Guest Services' desk and possibly wait in a line to get another card.

Attach your cruise card to your lanyard and then to yourself.

Do not forget your medications! Grab a pill box from the dollar store to sort your meds by day. Often, people take their actual prescription bottles.

Chapter 2 - PACKING TIPS & HINTS

You may get so busy having fun on a cruise you forget to take your meds. If there are no tiny hands around, leave the pill box sitting out in your cabin so you will not forget to take them.

There are rarely unforeseen circumstances on a ship. But it is wise to pack extra medications, snacks, etc. in case of an emergency at sea.

Keep your travel agent's number handy as well as numbers for your relatives and local hotels.

Also take along your medical ID card or an index card with all of your pertinent medical information on it. Allergies, blood type, medications, etcetera. Put your name, address, and emergency contacts on it.

The cruise line should have much of this information from when you booked your cruise. But it is always a great idea to keep one in your cabin as well.

Bring along some Post-It pads for notes you may need to leave other family members in your room. Dry erase markers work well on the mirrors too. Wipe it away with a Kleenex.

Remember, the walls of the cabin will be magnetic, so grab some magnets at the dollar store.

Cruise Control

You may be surprised at how much you will use the stickies or magnets. Suction hooks work well too.

In the Caribbean, the evenings are normally pleasant. However, in other places such as Alaska, Canada, Europe, and other areas, you will find the evenings can be moderately chilly. Take a small sweatshirt or jacket.

I pack a thin jacket even for the Caribbean because you never know what the weather will be like. It's a good idea to layer your clothes.

If you enjoy snorkeling, you may want to bring your mask and snorkel. If you do not have these, they can be rented on the beach for around $10-$20. Or your excursion guide will provide them.

You'll see people who prefer to bring their own snorkeling equipment due to not wanting to use one other people have used. However, they are sanitized and sterilized.

Cruise ships do not sell chewing gum. So, if you love to chew it, bring it.

Taking a small loofah is a good idea. We got sunburned on one cruise and had tiny blisters on our arms and backs. Looked funny, so we bought a small loofah in port to scrub with.

Chapter 2 - PACKING TIPS & HINTS

Take along a pair of tweezers. You might get an unruly eyebrow hair and need to snag it. Plus, they are a must for splinters.

You will have all the hand soap and lotion you will need supplied to you in your stateroom. I find these soaps and lotions drying, so I prefer to take my own. I buy those small, easy-to-pack bottles or fill my own tiny plastic bottles.

Another option I like is to take a liquid hand soap. Smells good! When I pack any liquids in my suitcase, I will double bag them in Ziplocs.

Your hair could get dry from the water if you spend more than a week on a ship. Though the ship supplies it, I also bring my own shampoo and conditioner.

There will be a blow dryer supplied in your room. And if it is not up to par, they will try to find you a better one.

A lot of people leave their priceless jewelry at home. If you do bring it, take along extra smoothie straws (the big ones) to feed your necklaces and bracelets through.

This is an ideal way to keep them from getting tangled up. And you will not misplace them in a drawer. Be sure not to inadvertently throw the straw away. Put them in the safe immediately.

Another great idea is to use a contact lens case (or two) to store smaller pieces such as earring studs. These cases are inexpensive and worth it to keep your smaller jewelry separated.

The only piece of valuable jewelry I take on cruises is my wedding ring, which does not leave my finger. The rest of what I take is beautiful, costume-type jewelry. You might be surprised at how costume jewelry makes dressy clothes look even better.

Those daily pill containers you get at the drug store also work great for jewelry storage. And the pill containers fit nicely in the safe in your cabin.

You may prefer to hang clothes instead of folding them and putting them in drawers. We prefer to hang ours, so we always take extra hangers. The ship will provide you more, but oftentimes, especially on long cruises, you won't have enough.

We sometimes take along a couple of those fold-up hangers. You can find these on-line and at Amazon.

Chapter 2 - PACKING TIPS & HINTS

Bungee cords or doorstops come in handy for propping doors open in your cabin. The balcony door sometimes will not stay open if you want it to (maybe to enjoy the beautiful views or smell the ocean). We have had this issue on several cruises we've been on.

Keep in mind when you leave your balcony door open (because you love the breeze and sound of the ocean), if there is a strong wind, the door can and likely will slam shut. Secure it! This is important for safety. You do not want to ruin your cruise with smashed fingers!

Don't forget your camera. I learned from another cruiser how smart it is to take extra SD cards and change it out every day in case you lose your camera. At least you'll still have the pictures on the SD card.

These days, people take photos with their cell phones. But I will be honest and say that I have lost pictures taken with my cell phone more than once.

If you are taking tours which include snorkeling type ventures, you may want to invest in an underwater camera. We have some fabulous pictures from an inexpensive Nikon underwater camera.

If you google "best underwater cameras," you will see some excellent cameras at reasonable prices.

Another idea is to upload your pictures to an album on Facebook or some other social media or even to a printer such as Walgreen's so the photos will be there should you lose your camera or phone.

Take along a couple sheets of bubble wrap in case you lose your camera bag. Great idea for any other delicate item you may need cushioning for too.

If you do not have one, you will want to invest in a backpack for your travels. When you go ashore, this will come in handy. You'll most likely want to take along water bottles and snacks. Or you may want to grab some souvenirs.

I always take a crossover purse to keep my hands free and so I will not have to be concerned with losing it.

B. LEAVE THESE AT HOME

You will get all types of different advice on what you can and cannot bring on board a ship.

Chapter 2 - PACKING TIPS & HINTS

The prudent thing to do is to look on-line and read the cruise line's policies regarding what you can and cannot bring on board their ship.

Items confiscated by the cruise line may be returned upon debarkation.

No firearms (or toys resembling real firearms) are permitted on board. The only exceptions are those who have permission from the ship's Captain, including law enforcement people and armed security guards working in an official capacity.

Toy weapons are not allowed. No explosive items, propellants, or flammable liquids. No pellet or BB guns.

Pretty much anything construed as a fire hazard is off limits. No coffeemakers. Bring your instant if you must and grab hot water from the buffet.

Shouldn't bring pool toys as these items could fly overboard. Also, no kites or drones.

No skateboards. No surfboards. No baseball bats.

We have seen people bring candy and granola bars on board. However, at the time of this writing, homemade edible items are not allowed. Nor are meats, fruits, or vegetables.

<u>Cruise Control</u>

Illegal drugs and the paraphernalia for them are, of course, prohibited.

With medical marijuana being prescribed these days, I'd check with the cruise line for whether you can take it. If you find you are allowed to take it on board, bring your prescription info with you for proof.

If you are caught with any illegal drugs, even one joint, you will be booted at the next port and presumably arrested. Drug-sniffing police K-9s will be taken to your cabin to search. Best to just not do it!

Can't bring any large scissors or knives on board. Some ships allow scissors of up to four inches long.

No pepper spray either. Leave it home.

Again, cigarette lighters are not permitted on ships.

No pets allowed on ships. If you have a service animal, ask the cruise line about restrictions. Be sure they are able to accommodate a service animal. You will likely need to provide the necessary documentation to prove it is a service animal.

Chapter 2 - PACKING TIPS & HINTS

There is a complete list on-line of banned items, what you cannot bring on board a ship. And if you get caught with one of these items, it will be confiscated and returned to you upon debarkation.

Chapter 3 – EMBARKATION DAY/BOARDING

A. ARRIVING AT THE PORT

Most cruise lines and/or ships will have an app. Download it before you leave home. This could be a lifesaver for you on your trip. The cruise line will likely have everything you need on their app.

Embarkation can be daunting. So, if you've never done it, read on for some idea of what it is like.

If you love to people watch, the cruise port is the place to do it. But try not to laugh out loud because people will be watching you too!

You will stand in line to check in. The line normally moves fast.

When you book your cruise, you will receive your luggage tags via email with your cabin number. You will need to tape or staple your tags to your luggage.

The baggage handlers will take your luggage straight to your cabin upon your arrival at the port. Don't forget to tip these porters.

Cruise Control

Paper tags may come loose from your luggage if you staple them. Some type of plastic luggage tags is the best way to go.

We always tape one of our business cards inside each piece of our luggage or even on the outside of it so there are two pieces of identification on the outside of the luggage.

I've seen people put them in their luggage tags as well. An extra piece of information is welcome by the baggage handlers in case yours gets misplaced.

Oftentimes, people will wait until they get in line at check-in to fill out their luggage tags. Don't do that. It keeps the line from moving. Fill them out when you get them.

A large number of bags look identical. Tie bright, bold ribbons or fabric pieces on the handles. Or try using a brightly-colored duct tape or fluorescent tape tied around part of the bags.

You could use some type of stickers, but they may peel off after the first use.

People sometimes purchase brightly-colored luggage, specifically so they will not have to try to find it in a mirage of other luggage.

Chapter 3 – EMBARKATION DAY/BOARDING

Your luggage may arrive to your cabin early or it may arrive later in the afternoon. Every bag put on the ship will go through a security scan.

After check-in, you will stand in line to go through security. Every passenger will go through a full-body metal detector. Every time you get on or off the ship in a port, you will, once again, proceed through a metal detector.

You *may* be assigned a group number. You will provide your cruise documents and passports at this time to the person at the counter. You will open your on-board account as well, either with a credit card or cash (if you did not open your account when you booked your cruise).

You are ready to board the ship. However, keep in mind cruise lines proceed with the process differently. I can honestly say we have rarely had to wait in long lines to board any ship.

After you take a number of cruises (this number is different for each cruise line), you will be given what is called Priority Boarding, meaning you will bypass others and get right on the ship.

Some cruise lines even let you select your own boarding time when you book your cruise. Get on

Cruise Control

your ship as soon as you can as you will have a buffet and other dining options waiting for you.

Oftentimes, the elevators will be closed during the embarkation process due to the thousands of pieces of luggage they are trying to deliver to the cabins. You will need to take stairs to get to where you're going.

However, for mobility impaired individuals, oftentimes the elevators at either end of the ship will be working.

The pool area may be extremely busy during embarkation, so prepare for lots of people. You will want to grab one of the pool chairs quickly.

If you get on board early, you can be at the pool, umbrella drink in hand, while others are still trying to get on the ship. And your children can be grabbing some soft-serve ice cream served on nearly all ships.

The general rule with cruise lines is every person should be on the ship two hours before departure.

A great tip is to take a selfie on your phone and camera before you board the ship. If you should misplace either item, you will have no trouble

Chapter 3 – EMBARKATION DAY/BOARDING

identifying it as yours. You will have your identification right there on it.

You will also have your picture made when you check in to get your cruise under way. This picture is electronically attached to your cruise card. Every time you leave the ship or get back on the ship, this card will be inserted into a machine where security will verify it is you.

B. WHAT TO BRING IN CARRY-ON BAG

You are allowed to bring a carry-on bag with you, so pack what you may need before your luggage arrives.

The luggage handlers will deliver your big luggage to your cabin, but you need a smaller bag with a swimsuit, sunscreen, sunglasses, money, camera, your meds, or any other item you may need as you will want to commence your fun the moment you board the ship.

You'll see people wear their bathing suits under their clothes so they can head straight to the pool.

Some people put the clothes they will wear to dinner in their carry-on in case their luggage gets lost during delivery to the cabins. We have never done this and have never had our luggage lost.

Cruise Control

You might consider using a beach bag with a cooler on the bottom for your carry-on bag. Convenient for drinks or snacks.

Be sure to put a luggage tag on your carry-on. If you misplace it, you will likely see it in your cabin later the same day.

Keep your cruise documents, including your cruise card, and passport or photo ID, with you on embarkation day.

Packing these important documents in luggage out of your possession is not a good idea. You may find your luggage going on a cruise of its own while you are stuck ashore if you do not keep your documents with you.

Luggage rarely gets misplaced, but it can happen. Do not forget to keep your meds with you until the minute you get into your cabin.

Keep in mind, pieces of luggage look identical. It is a great idea to take a picture of your luggage for this reason. Staff will have the picture of it and can search specifically for your piece(s).

You will need to check with the particular cruise line you book through, but most ships will allow you to bring on at least one bottle of wine or

Chapter 3 – EMBARKATION DAY/BOARDING

champagne. Though you may be able to find one on the ship, you may want to bring a corkscrew!

When you embark on your journey and when you debark, there will be porters walking the terminal, ready and more than willing to help you with your luggage. Let them help you. Work as little as possible on your vacation!

It is customary to tip these ladies and gentlemen for their help. Utilizing this help will get you on the ship to commence your vacation and off the ship headed for home much quicker.

We have found our luggage is delivered to our cabin shortly after boarding. However, they ask you allow them until late in the afternoon, as they have thousands of pieces of luggage to deliver to the cabins.

We unpack our luggage as soon as it is delivered to our cabin. We want to get unpacking out of the way and get going with our fun! Plus, it only takes 10 or 15 minutes to unpack!

After you unpack your stuff, store your luggage under the bed, out of the way. Then go enjoy yourself on the trip of a lifetime!

<u>Cruise Control</u>

On most cruise lines, not all, every member of your group is allowed to bring on a 12-pack of soda or juice.

We have found most often no bottled water is allowed to be brought on board.

Please check on-line for the individual cruise line's rules. These rules do periodically change, and we have seen times when you can bring a limited amount of water on board.

You could also take refillable water bottles. This will save money if you are a big water drinker, like me. The water on board is perfectly safe. They, of course, have a state-of-the-art filtration system.

If you are flying to your cruise port to board the ship, keep in mind you cannot carry liquids on board flights.

C. BOARDING THE SHIP

We make it a habit of attempting to learn the layout of the ship shortly after we board. We try to remember which way to go, left or right, coming out of our cabin to get to wherever we are going.

Chapter 3 – EMBARKATION DAY/BOARDING

When we first started cruising, we spent plenty of time trying to find places, looking for bathrooms, etcetera. Try to learn the layout of the ship.

You may find getting from one end of the ship to the other end is easier in the long hallways where cabins are located. It is much less crowded. This is true for the duration of your trip as well.

Some ships do not stop elevator service during embarkation. But the elevators will likely be packed when you board the ship.

Take the stairs, especially if you are in a hurry. It's a great idea to take the stairs during the duration of your trip!

One of the best views you will see is leaving port after embarkation. Take your camera and head to the upper decks. This is where most people on board will go to see the ship sail away. The music will be great, the breeze will be great, the views will be great.

Oftentimes, the shops on the ship will be offering great deals for the first day. Head there after you set sail if you're looking for great deals.

Though there are excellent sales in the shops on the ships, you may save yourself even more money if you check on Amazon for the exact product you are interested in.

If your ship has one, head to the zip line after embarkation before it gets too crowded during the rest of your trip and you have to wait in a line. This is often an extra cost.

Keep in mind, zip lining is sometimes one of the offered excursions at various ports. We have zip-lined at several different locations and loved it!

After the ship sets sail, head to the main dining room and find your assigned table for the duration of your voyage. If you do not like the location, you can request a change. They are there to make your trip perfect and will not mind at all changing your table.

Before the ship sets sail or shortly after it sets sail, you will be required to attend a muster drill (also known as a lifeboat drill or safety drill).

This is an important drill required by the International Maritime Organization. Everyone is required to attend.

You will be requested to assemble in a certain part of the ship such as a lounge or common area to

Chapter 3 – EMBARKATION DAY/BOARDING

receive the instructions on what to do in the event of a disaster.

Don't try to skip this drill. They take head counts, and you will be required to attend it the next day if you skip out on the first day.

This drill is for your own safety and lasts about 20 minutes. Pay attention to what they are saying.

You will hear seven *loud* blasts of the ship's horn followed by one horn blast. Make your little ones aware of this so they will not be alarmed.

On the latest ships we've cruised on, the guests were not required to take their life jacket to the drill. You will have life jackets in your cabin for every person staying in the room.

The elevators are normally off during this drill. So, you may want to head to your muster station 30 minutes ahead of time if you want to take the elevator.

If you are handicapped or need assistance walking, ask your cabin steward or the Guest Relations Desk for help.

On the first or second night, the staff will participate in a Welcome Aboard show in the main

Cruise Control

show lounge. I advise going to this, especially if this is your first cruise, as you will gain a wealth of knowledge about cruising and your cruise ship.

D. ON-BOARD PHOTOS

As you board the ship, there will be photographers standing by to take your picture. The next day, these photos will be posted in the designated photo display area.

Ship photographers are plentiful, especially in the evenings. They offer photo packages, which can be advantageous if you are trying not to spend too much while on your trip.

People have differing opinions on the cost of the pictures taken by the ship's photographers. I have found them to be a reasonable price. However, I have heard from others they are outrageously priced.

They will take your picture upon arrival on the ship and every time you leave the ship in port.

Formal night pictures are beautiful and fun to take.

Your photo will be taken countless times during your cruise, oftentimes in front of beautiful

Chapter 3 – EMBARKATION DAY/BOARDING

backdrops, and will be displayed on a daily basis in the photo area and left there during the duration of your cruise.

On ships these days, you may see the photos on computer kiosks. You simply let them know which one(s) you want, they will print them.

You retrieve your pictures in the photo area, or they will deliver them to your cabin. Super easy!

It's a great idea to wait until the last evening to pick out the best pictures out of all of your pictures. This is an excellent way not to overspend on photos.

Be sure to ask about this in the photo area, however, as not all ships keep all pictures until the end of the cruise. The photo kiosks definitely store your pictures until the end.

We have found the sizes of their pictures are sometimes not standard sizes. You may have to trim your photos or purchase custom frames when you get back home.

Some cruisers pose for every professional picture they can. Then they pick the best ones out of the lot. You do not have to purchase any picture you do not want.

<u>Cruise Control</u>

Fellow cruisers are usually happy to take a picture for you and your family. We have never had anyone refuse to take our picture.

Cruisers are generally truly friendly people and excited to be on vacation. They help out others with taking pictures because at some point during the cruise, they will likely ask another cruiser to take their picture.

If you see someone trying to get a group photo or couple's photo, offer to take it for them. They will likely reciprocate by taking yours.

If you see another cruiser taking a selfie or a photograph of their family, be sure to stay out of their way!

If you are in a location where you want to take a number of photos in the same spot, such as with the ship in the background, move over and let the other people walk on by. Common courtesy.

You will see passengers obsessed with taking photos, using selfie sticks and such. Try to have patience and remember they are on vacation having a grand time, like you. They are trying to capture moments of their trip, like you will be. Niceness always works best.

Chapter 4 – LIFE ON BOARD THE SHIP

A. DRESS

You only need to unpack your clothes one time! Who could ask for more?

The clothes you pack will, of course, depend upon your destination.

Before you leave on your dream vacation, google the weather conditions for the ports you will be headed to. I have listed in this book items you will need no matter what your destination is.

On board your ship, most of the time, shorts and casual shirts/T-shirts are appropriate, especially if you choose to eat in the buffet.

For the restaurants, they prefer no one wear shorts or cutoffs. You are not allowed to wear flip-flops in the dining room. However, sandals are allowed.

Dinner in the dining room is smart casual wear such as slacks or skirts with dressy tops or dresses. Men normally wear casual slacks, casual shirts, and oftentimes a sports jacket. A jacket is not necessary though.

Cruise Control

There are customarily two formal nights on seven-day cruises. Guests love to get dressy and show off their finest attire.

If you do not own a tux, that's okay. Suits are perfectly acceptable. You can rent a tux on board.

A great number of people choose not to dress up. That's one of the wonderful things about cruising. You can go with the flow, or not.

On formal night, you will find most, not all, people in the main dining room will be dressed formally. So, you may want to head to the buffet for the evening meal if you choose not to dress up.

The formal evenings are fun, a chance to wear your beautiful evening gown and tux or suit. There will be a band playing in the atrium with dancing and everyone sitting around having a grand time. Always fun to people watch and see what everyone wears.

When we first started cruising, I would pack everything I could fit into our luggage. And I start my list of what we need to take about three weeks before we depart. This assures me I will not forget anything (usually).

I have made a packing list over the years. And I normally have something to add after every trip.

Chapter 4 – LIFE ON BOARD THE SHIP

Every time we take a trip, I use this list to make sure we have everything we need.

These days when we cruise, I pack light, handwash items (if needed) and wear them more than once. We are less stressed not dragging tons of luggage around the airport and cruise terminal.

Try to pack light, as cruise ship cabins are not large (unless you book a suite). You can wear an item more than once. There are Laundromats available on board. Or handwash an item you've already worn and hang it in your cabin to dry.

Unless you are traveling to cold destinations, it is sufficient to bring along a light jacket or a sweater. In lots of locations, it tends to get breezy at night.

Oftentimes, the theater, restaurants, and all the other air-conditioned places on the ship can get chilly.

If you are not cruising to a cold location, pack light fabrics such as rayon, silk, and polyester. These tend to occupy much less space in luggage. Mix and match your colors so you are able to pack less.

We've sometimes packed an empty tote bag in case we found one or two items on our trip we simply couldn't live without!

<u>Cruise Control</u>

You do not have to pack beach towels as the ship provides them. You are allowed to take the ship towels on shore at ports. You may be charged if you do not return the ship's towel.

There is a product called compression bags some people use for packing.

These bags squeeze out all the air as you pack your belongings, allowing you to put more in your suitcase. I have never used these, but I have seen others have success with them.

Try putting a dryer sheet in each of your suitcases to keep your clothes smelling fresh and help with static cling. We've done it. It works!

The one and only time you may need dressy shoes is on formal night. And honestly, I have worn sort-of dressy sandals with a formal dress.

There have been formal nights where we decided to forego dressing fancy and chose to walk around dressed in our casual clothes. Again, this is perfectly acceptable.

You may be able to check your cruise pre-departure documents on their website to see if there are any themed nights such as '70s night, western night, Mardi Gras evening, etcetera. Or call

Chapter 4 – LIFE ON BOARD THE SHIP

the cruise line's customer service number and they may be able to tell you.

Over-packing is one of the biggest mistakes of travelers. Again, you might mix and match the color scheme of your wardrobe so you will be able to pack less. Pack versatile pieces matching several outfits.

And don't forget, if you overpack your luggage, the airline will charge you extra.

A tip I discovered from a fellow passenger is to roll your belts and store them in the collar of shirts. Not only does this help with space in luggage, but it also helps keep the collars nice and in place.

There are duty-free shops on board to purchase whatever clothes you may need. Duty-free means you will not pay local tax. You may find some duty-free shops in ports as well.

I do not advise purchasing any electronics duty-free. If you have an issue with the electronic you bought, you may have a difficult time holding the company to the warranty or mailing the item back to the retailer.

When you are shopping in ports, you may not know exactly the price you are paying for an item if you do not know the currency exchange.

Cruise Control

You can always download the previously-mentioned app, XE Currency, on your phone for converting currency.

If you will be doing a lot of walking, as is the case in ports across the world, don't forget your tennis shoes or some other comfortable walking shoes!

You might consider bringing water shoes on your cruise. These are great shoes for walking around the pools, for walking in sand, rocky terrain, and the like.

Personally, I think it's a great idea to pack your shoes in some type of canvas bag or other type of bag before you pack them in your suitcase. I've seen some pretty icky, dirty, sandy shoes on cruises.

Before you leave on your fabulous journey, it is always a good idea to check the clothing requirements for the destinations you are going to.

Cultures are different in various areas of the world, requiring certain dress. There may be some you are unaware of.

For example, in some areas, you will need to have your shoulders covered. Other areas, you are expected to have your hair covered. You may not like it, but it is their country and you could be barred from entry if you do not comply.

Chapter 4 – LIFE ON BOARD THE SHIP

Some countries such as Europe are not too keen on sloppy casual wear such as short shorts and T-shirts.

Again, research this information on-line before you head out on your trip.

When you are packing to head out for the fabulous time you are about to have, don't pack too tightly. Leave some space in your luggage for souvenirs or any other beautiful item (like a gorgeous sweater) you might find to purchase.

B. KIDS' CLUBS

These free clubs are typically for youngsters ages 3-17. There is sometimes a separate Teens' Club. The kids enjoy being in these clubs, making new friends and being away from Mom and Dad.

Upon embarkation, you will likely see staff from these clubs standing there waiting to greet your children.

I have never taken small kiddos on a cruise, but I have been told the Kids' Clubs take children younger than 3 for a slight charge. You may want to research this if you have toddlers.

Cruise Control

There are ships which offer child care after 6:00 p.m. for a nominal charge. We've been on ships where in-room child care was offered as well.

These are interactive and well-organized programs. Some of them are late-night programs, allowing the parents to enjoy shows, dancing, etcetera.

It's a prudent idea to visit the Kids' Club and speak with the program directors. I have never heard anything negative about these Kids' Clubs, but I personally would feel much more comfortable about sending my kids off if I knew what they were getting into.

The ships have teen programs as well as Kids' Clubs. The younger kiddos, tweens and teens have their own places to hang out on ships.

What an awesome opportunity for them to mingle with other teens from all over the world! And what a great learning experience!

Most ships have teen discos. If you want to appear super old, walk into one of these. Ugh! Your teens are perfectly safe in these discos or any other place on the ship.

Chapter 4 – LIFE ON BOARD THE SHIP

You can be assured there are security cameras on board every ship in all public areas.

Again, these venues for children of all ages are free with the exception of child care for babies.

C. CELL PHONES

As much as we want to get away and relax on the beautiful seas, we hate to not have our connection with social media.

The ship will have an Internet plan, but it may be slow and expensive. If you make a call or log on to social media and you do not have a plan in place, expect to pay $15 to $30 or more per call or log-in.

Are you sure you can't do without checking on Facebook and Pinterest? After all, you are trying to relax.

When you are not using your cell phone, it should be powered off or at least in airplane mode. The charges will be large if you do not turn off roaming. Texting can sometimes be less expensive than calling.

When you are traveling internationally, ask your carrier about an International Plan they may have. This will be much less expensive.

Do not forget your portable charger for your phone. You may be off the ship at a port and run out of battery. We keep our cell phones charging in our cabin at night.

Oftentimes, ships offer discounts and free minutes if you purchase the Internet package on the first day of your cruise. However, the Internet tends to run notably slow on ships.

There are sometimes Internet cafes in port crew members can provide you information for. They will know where the best Wi-Fi areas are on land as well. They tend to use these to stay in touch with their families.

D. FREEBIES & DISCOUNTS

Many people automatically conclude cruises are extremely expensive. They can be and they may not be.

If you are not a drinker of alcohol, you will have close to zero expenses other than excursions and professional portraits on board.

In fact, I have listed a litany of freebies below available on most ships.

Chapter 4 – LIFE ON BOARD THE SHIP

Your ship will have a shopping lecture on the first or second day after you set sail. It is customarily in the main theater.

They oftentimes throw freebies such as T-shirts out to the crowd. Some of these freebies are super nice.

If you miss the shopping lecture, you will find it on your TV playing repeatedly every day.

There are tons of free, on-board activities giving you a chance of winning prizes. I've listed a number of those activities in this book.

There are dance lessons such as Zumba, bartending classes, towel folding demonstrations (where they teach you how to fold towels into the small animals the steward leaves on your bed every night).

You may see art classes or flower arranging classes on board. How about classes to teach you the fine art of making cocktails? You'll likely see some. All free!

You may see free knitting or crochet classes.

I will never forget this. One of the best times I have ever had on a ship was watching the glass-blowing! They went through the whole process, showing guests exactly how to do it. Amazing talent and what an awesome time!

The demonstration was outside, and it was freezing as we headed to Alaska. But beautiful glassware!

There are art auctions where they generally offer free wine or champagne. You do not have to buy a thing, simply show up. You may be given a piece of art for attending.

On cruise ships, you will see beautiful artwork. Though it is normally an auction, you can also buy outright.

It is probable you did not take a cruise to buy art. Again, keep in mind free champagne is served at these art galleries. Careful not to overindulge and decide you must have a piece of artwork.

Aside from possibly spending more than you planned to, you will be responsible for getting it back home.

Now do not get me wrong. As mentioned above, the art is beautiful. However, be careful with the sales tactics, and research what you are told.

Chapter 4 – LIFE ON BOARD THE SHIP

Continuing on with freebies and discounts….

If you are in a group where beer is the drink of choice, you will save money buying a bucket of beer rather than a beer at a time.

If you have cruised the same cruise line before, the ship may have a welcome back party or past guest party where you are offered free drinks and appetizers.

After your cruise is over, fill out the comment card for a chance to win a free cruise.

There is customarily a Captain's Cocktail Party on each ship. Sometimes you are required to have a personal invitation. Other times, everyone is invited. There are *free* drinks and hors d'oeuvres served at these parties.

If there is a timeshare presentation on board, go to it. You do not have to buy into the timeshare to receive possible cash, onboard credits, or tickets to shows.

Oftentimes, ships will have liquor tasting events. Normally, there is a slight charge for these events.

Visit the ship's shops. You will have days on your cruise when the gift shops on board have excellent sales! Grab your souvenirs. You will find gold-by-the-inch at reasonable prices, but keep in mind this is gold-plated jewelry.

In a large number of these shops, you will find name brand clothes, perfumes of all brands, purses of all brands, including Coach and Michael Kors, as well as Rolex watches and other designer watches such as Pandora, Movado, TAG Heuer, Longines and Citizen.

Unless there's a special restaurant in the port you are visiting, hop back on the ship for lunch. You'll find all the free food you can eat.

Spa use on ships is typically not free, but you can receive deep discounts on embarkation day and on port days. The steam rooms and saunas can generally be used for free.

Also, as the ship starts sailing, the spa will try to fill spots for the length of the cruise. Typically, you can find specials daily during your cruise.

You can book any spa treatments (and some ships have beauty salons, even barber shops) on-line before your cruise begins. This is a wonderful idea if you want to utilize this service for formal night.

Chapter 4 – LIFE ON BOARD THE SHIP

Ask the crew in the spa what specials they will be having during your voyage. Most cruise ships offer free tours of their beautiful spa facilities. You will likely find steam rooms and saunas in the spa area *free* of charge.

Free room service is available on most (I believe) ships. It's been available on every ship we've been on. There may be a minimal service charge, especially on late-night orders.

The menus are generally limited but still excellent. Room service is a great idea if you need to leave the ship early in the morning for a tour in port.

You will find a free sports area on most ships. Basketball, table tennis, dodgeball, volleyball, chess, miniature golf, shuffleboard, and other sports.

The Cruise Director will likely organize free sports competitions. If you are the competitive type, you'll enjoy these!

Miniature golf is always relaxing and always fun. It will be located on one of the top decks of the ship out in the open air free of charge (on every ship we've been on).

Cruise Control

We have not been on a ship with a golf simulator, but we have heard of them being on some ships and being lots of fun.

How about attending one of the informative *free* seminars on board? Acupuncture, art, napkin folding, making sushi, weight loss.

Or you may be interested in one of the numerous ongoing bingo games every day on board. These are not free, but you could win cash (and lots of it sometimes) or a free cruise! Yep, a free cruise! We have seen people win one on every cruise we've been on!

If you are averse to bingo, you are allowed to go in and sit and enjoy. And sometimes it gets downright comical!

The bingo games on board are either the punch-out cards or the boppers. You will ordinarily be required to purchase the boppers.

If you participate in the contests on board or volunteer for certain activities, you may win key chains, a plastic ship (woo-hoo), T-shirts, luggage tags, a bottle of wine, penlights, tote bags, cups and mugs, free drinks, all kinds of things.

Chapter 4 – LIFE ON BOARD THE SHIP

An extra benefit for participating is you'll meet lots of new people!

Did you know if you have a large group of people traveling together, most cruise lines give large discounts?

Not only might you receive discounts, but oftentimes, cruise lines offer extra perks for group travel such as cabin upgrades and shipboard credits.

Check with the individual cruise lines for the benefits of traveling as a large group.

It may be wise to use a travel agent if you have a large group. They will work hard to find the best possible deal for your group.

I advise having one designated person in your group to correspond with the travel agent. The best travel agent to have is one specializing in group travel.

Communicate with your agent if you have a large group to plan travel for, such as wedding parties, family reunions and the like.

Some cruise lines have specific packages for large groups such as free cabins or even free cruises. This can be a great savings.

Cruise Control

You'll see ships offering free tours of the galley. I highly recommend this. It is fascinating and fun to see the cooking area they use to prepare food for thousands.

The larger ships these days have upwards of 5,000-6,000 passengers. Can you imagine cooking for this many? Nope! These cooks prepare anywhere from 15,000 to 30,000 (or more) meals per day!

You may be surprised to learn the galley area is cleaned and sanitized after each mealtime. At least half, if not more, of the ship's staff work in the food and beverage area.

Tours of the galley are super popular tours, so you may need to book the galley tour ahead of time, such as when you book your cruise.

Did you know open flames are not allowed on ships? Me either. Learned it on a tour of the galley we took. They do use tiny torches for certain desserts.

If you are on your honeymoon, shout it out to everyone. Be loud and clear about it. You will receive all kinds of freebies and perks if certain staff members hear you.

Chapter 4 – LIFE ON BOARD THE SHIP

If you have enjoyed your cruise vacation so much you cannot wait to take another one, head to the desk provided specifically for you to book your next cruise. It's like putting a cruise in layaway.

Plus, if you join the cruise line's VIP list, you will build points, earning perks such as priority check-in (no lines), priority boarding and debarkation, special luggage handling, deals on the ship, etcetera.

This is immensely appealing when 4,000 people (or more) are trying to get on or off a ship.

E. DRINK PACKAGES & ON-BOARD BEVERAGES

Your cruise may offer what is called an Unlimited Drink Package. You will lock in the cost of your beverages. This is a per-day cost.

I'm not sure if this is the case with all cruise lines, but on the ships we have been on, if one person in the cabin purchases a drink package, the others must purchase it as well. This can make these drink packages costly.

Before purchasing this package, be sure to consider the length of your cruise as well as the number of days you are in port where you may get less value for this drink package (as you may not be on the ship while in port).

You are able to purchase these drink packages when you book your cruise or after you have boarded the ship. If you purchase one, you will not have a hefty drink bill at the end of your cruise.

The beverage package for sodas may be beneficial if you have children traveling with you. You receive unlimited refills, and the packages are ordinarily in the $40 range (as of this writing).

Most ships allow you to bring a limited number of beverages on board with you. Check your cruise line's web site for their rule on this.

There are no rules on board about where you can take beverages. You can take a beverage from the dining room to the pool, from the bar to the show, from the casino to the spa.

No matter what you are drinking, be it an adult beverage or a Coke, you can carry it with you wherever you go.

You are also allowed to take a plate of food anywhere you want to.

Chapter 4 – LIFE ON BOARD THE SHIP

On most cruises we've been on, if you order tea, coffee, or water at the pool, you will be charged. Walk to the buffet area (very close to the pool area anyway) and get your own non-alcoholic beverage. It's free there! You can even get juice there.

The above is also true for bar areas. You will be charged for non-alcoholic drinks.

Go to the water fountain and refill your own water bottle!

As I previously mentioned, attend the cocktail parties you may be invited to. You will receive free drinks and hors d'oeuvres there.

People enjoy having a glass of wine for each dinner. You can purchase a whole bottle and have the waiter mark the bottle with your name and cabin number. You will be given your exact wine from your purchased bottle every time you order a glass of wine, if you so choose.

Most ships will have a drink of the day every day. These are served in souvenir glasses you can keep.

If you like the Drink of the Day, instead of paying for another souvenir glass, ask for a refill in the same glass. Or ask for the drink of the day in a regular glass, not a souvenir glass.

<u>Cruise Control</u>

F. DINING ON BOARD

You will find some of the best cuisine in the world on cruise ships. You will find extensive wine lists, exquisite meats, fresh vegetables, and simply sublime desserts.

There are few, if any, people who do not overindulge. Can't pass on the superb food!

There will not be a shortage of food on your ship. You will have any number of restaurants included in the cost of your cruise. Bistros, hamburgers, buffets, sushi bars, pizza bars, etcetera, each having super friendly, helpful waiters waiting on you.

You will find anything from snacks to full-course, healthy, delicious meals.

You get to choose your diet while on board. You can over-indulge on delicious fattening food or eat healthy, low-fat, gluten-free, or vegetarian.

There is a charge for the specialty restaurants on ships, but the fabulous food is well worth it.

There are also specialty coffee shops on a good number of ships. The coffee is an extra charge, but they serve delicious pastries, and they're customarily *free*!

Chapter 4 – LIFE ON BOARD THE SHIP

When we started cruising 28 years ago, everything was free, even the steak dinners. We have concluded over time, the food in the dining room has been upgraded and options are limitless.

Depending on the length of your cruise, you may get burned out on the ship's food. So, you may want to research restaurants at your ports of call ahead of time.

If you have any food allergies, are vegetarian, if you avoid red meat, are gluten-free, or have any kind of special requests or food requirements, let your headwaiter know.

They will make sure your dining room experience is superb. They will go out of their way to assure you have what you need.

When we first started cruising, you could not pre-book your dining preferences. Today, it is much more convenient.

You can reserve a table at the specialty restaurants on most ships and receive a discount if you book three or more dining reservations.

Children 6 – 12 receive discounts at these restaurants as well. Children 5 and under customarily dine for free in specialty restaurants.

<u>Cruise Control</u>

On the first night of your cruise, you may find nice discounts in these specialty restaurants.

The food in the main dining room is excellent, so we rarely eat in one of the specialty restaurants.

You can have seconds or thirds in the main dining room if you wish. You can have two desserts or two entrees if you wish.

If you ordered something you are not happy with, let your waiter know. They are more than happy to bring you whatever you want. Your satisfaction is what they want. They strive to appease you!

If you had something the previous night you found especially delicious, ask for it again on another night. Because it may not be on the menu does not mean they do not have it available!

If you do not care for anything on the specialty dining menu for a specific evening, ask your waiter for the regular menu where you will find steak, chicken, or fish (just maybe not so fancy). But delicious!

Something people do not know is you can obtain a main dining room menu for the duration of your trip at the Guest Services' desk. Great way to help you decide if you prefer to eat in the main dining

Chapter 4 – LIFE ON BOARD THE SHIP

room on certain evenings or go to one of the specialty restaurants on board.

The menus are posted outside the door of the restaurants as well.

You will find the food in the specialty restaurants delicious! And the prices are reasonable.

In the main dining room, you have a choice of having either a set dining time or what they call anytime dining.

We always go with the anytime dining because we never know what we will be doing and when we will be doing it. By the time we decide to take a vacation, we are trying to break away from schedules!

If you choose the set dining time, you will have the same waitstaff and sit at the same table every night for dinner. You will also sit with the same people assigned seating table.

The waitstaff is excellent, always trying to make your eating experience the best.

The two set dining times are what they call early dining and late dining. These times are, of course, different on every ship. But we have customarily found these times to be 6:00 p.m. and 8:15 p.m.

If you are on your honeymoon (or for any other reason) and prefer to sit at a table alone, you can request a table to yourself, and the staff will comply.

You may choose to enjoy your dining experience out in the open, under the beautiful sky and stars.

Don't want lunch at the Lido buffet again? Try having lunch in the main dining room. It is fabulous!

On most ships we have been on, an adult may order from the children's menu and a child may order from the adult menu.

Oh, no! You're going to be late for the show? Ask for your dessert to be boxed so you can take it with you!

Or maybe you want a late-night snack. Ask for a dessert to take back to your cabin with you. The waitstaff wants to make you happy!

If you find you are not happy with the folks you are assigned to sit with, you are free to ask to be assigned to another table. The waitstaff will be glad to move you.

Chapter 4 – LIFE ON BOARD THE SHIP

We have met some genuinely nice people at our table with the assigned seating arrangement. On the other end of that, we have met people who've helped us choose not to go back to a specific table.

No need to make your vacation miserable having to sit there with bumps on a log. You do not have to! Ask for another table.

If you do choose the assigned seating in the main dining room, try not to be late. The waiter customarily waits for everyone to show before they start service.

If you are not going to be there or you will be late, it is common courtesy to let the waiter or your tablemates know.

When you eat in the main dining room for breakfast or lunch, you are at liberty to sit where you would like to.

G. CHOOSE TO BE CONSIDERATE

(make your cruise enjoyable and memorable)

On cruise ships with upwards of 5,000-6,000 (even more) passengers, it is inevitable someone may get on your nerves. It is all but a guarantee someone will exhibit what is annoying behavior to you.

Cruise Control

Cruises are supposed to be *fun*, relaxing getaways. But be sure to board the ship with an extra dose of *patience* and *tolerance*.

There could be several hundred different nationalities among the employees on a ship. However, most all will speak English. Please be kind to these employees. They are there to make your trip enjoyable.

You will also find various nationalities in your fellow cruisers. Again, please choose to be kind to everyone (and it is a choice)!

There are few things worse on a ship than being surrounded by drunk people. It is inevitable they will be around, but simply move on to another location.

Everyone is on the ship to relax and have fun. But try not to be one of those obnoxious people who do not know when to stop with the alcohol. This type of cruiser will get a reputation among fellow guests!

The comedy shows will be funny, but there could be people who laugh as loud as they can at everything the comedian says, even the not-so-funny stuff. They may talk loudly during the show. They may become annoying to the other guests.

Chapter 4 – LIFE ON BOARD THE SHIP

You do not want to be one of those drunk, obnoxious, noisy people in the shows.

If you are on your honeymoon, please remember you have a cabin for….well, that. Next to drinking too much, the most annoying situation we've seen (rarely seen) is couples who make out right in public, no matter who is around.

There is, of course, nothing wrong with holding hands or pecking on the cheek or lips, but if you need to make out no matter where you are, you could get a reputation around the ship and people will avoid you.

We have been on cruises when people knew when the loudest person on the cruise was coming. Everywhere they strolled they were talking loud and over everyone else.

And if they have a problem with something such as the wrong drink being brought to them, they will get even louder. These people will not have favorable reputations around the ship among the guests and staff.

You will meet a lot of people on a cruise. Again, bring an extra dose of patience with you and tolerate the unexpected.

Cruise Control

You want to be remembered as a kind and considerate person on this vacation, not a heckler or a Mr. Know It All.

When you get thousands of people together, it is inevitable you will run into rude, hateful people who refuse to be nice. Pass them by and continue to smile and be your happy self. Be glad you're not them and move on.

The ship as a whole will be noisy and full of happy people. However, there are certain areas designated as quiet areas. There may be an adults-only retreat area, perhaps called The Solarium.

There is the chapel, the library, the spa. There are places to get all the quiet you want.

Other ways you may find quiet times could be walking around the upper deck late at night or early in the morning. You can hear a pin drop and watch the beautiful ocean waves! Maybe get lucky enough to see whales, flying fish, or a group of dolphins!

There will be a large number of lounges around the ship. During their closed times, you are still allowed to go inside. All the peace and quiet you want! Sit and read a book.

Chapter 4 – LIFE ON BOARD THE SHIP

This goes without saying (but I'm going to say it anyway), there are NO circumstances under which you should sit or stand on the railing of a ship. The chances of them finding you if you fall overboard are *less than slim*.

Even if you are a tightrope walker, don't do it. Even if you've had too much to drink, that's not an excuse either!

You may be famished, but under no circumstances should you cut in line (if there is one) at the buffet. This will get you a dreadful reputation among other passengers, something you do not want.

While this is not entirely enforced by the ship's staff, it is rude to save the pool loungers if you are not going to use them. If you will be gone longer than, say, 30 minutes, take your items with you and let others enjoy the pool area in the comfort of a lounger.

Same is true of chairs in the show lounges. If you do not know for sure but *think* someone is going to join you, people will not look kindly on you for holding or reserving empty seats if they are the ones looking for a seat.

<u>Cruise Control</u>

My own personal opinion is 30 minutes tops for holding or reserving a seat at the pool, in the restaurants, or in the show lounges.

There will be people who do not agree with this, but there are those who consider it rude if you do not let people off elevators before getting on. Wait your turn to get on the elevator.

Some people will take the stairs if they are only going one floor, or two. If someone pushes the button to go one floor, brush it off and have fun anyway.

It is considerate to take the stairs if you are only going one or two decks. Everyone may not be considerate. Be kind anyway.

In the huge ships, the elevators get used a bunch. Try to take stairs if you can.

If someone is running to catch the elevator, hold the door open for them. You may see this person again during your trip, and they may return the favor.

It is all but guaranteed there will be someone who tries to cram into a full elevator on your trip. Try to have patience and politely say *we are full*.

Chapter 4 – LIFE ON BOARD THE SHIP

If you don't say that, people (no matter what size they are) will try to sneak in. We've seen it on most every cruise we've been on.

If it irks you, politely say *excuse me*, get off the elevator and wait for the next one. No need to cause a stink. You're not in *that* big of a hurry, are you? I personally hate crowded elevators anyway!

You are not allowed to have any type of candle in your room. Nor are you allowed to smoke in your room. Cruise lines want to limit smoking on board due to fire potential.

Even cigarette ash is a fire hazard. You do not want to be at sea if something catches fire on a ship.

I am not a smoker, but I do know there are designated smoking areas on all ships we have been on so far. I believe every ship has several specified areas, inside and outside, for smokers.

If you are able to get a blow dryer on board (they are not allowed) and plug it into the shaving outlet in the cabin bathroom, you may damage the blow dryer and possibly blow a fuse or ignite a fire. Don't do it.

The walls in your cabin are thin. If you have loud hanky-panky or have an argument with your

Cruise Control

roommate, your next-door neighbors will likely hear everything if they are in their cabin.

Try to keep the volume low on everything, unless it's okay with you if your neighbors hear too. Then they may complain.

Be careful when you get out of the shower or walk out of the bathroom. Though your steward will knock on the door before entering, you will likely not hear it if you are in the shower.

It is a good idea to hang the Do Not Disturb sign on the outside of your cabin door while you're showering.

If you have children on your cruise who are in the Kids' Club, there will still be times when they will be with you. Your fellow cruisers will be grateful if you keep control of your kiddos at all times when they are with you.

If they get out of hand, doing things such as pushing all the elevator buttons upon entering the elevator or running through those long hallways, you will get a reputation on the ship for having the most unruly, worst kids.

Please be considerate of your fellow cruisers. It is common courtesy to control your children.

Chapter 4 – LIFE ON BOARD THE SHIP

Do your best to be on time to any show, dinner, or any other activity. It is annoying to other passengers if they have to wait on someone who is notorious for being late. You may disrupt the entire event if they have to stop and wait until you take your seat.

Plus, if you're late, you may get called out by the comedian or whoever, even brought on stage to be jokingly made fun of. All in good fun!

If you do get annoyed about something during your vacation, speak to the Guest Services' desk or call security.

Remember you are there to have fun and enjoy yourself. Don't let others ruin your cruise vacation.

Security on your ship has the authority to do whatever needs to be done to make sure cruisers are safe. If you are unruly or obnoxious with other cruisers complaining about you, you could find yourself unable to board the ship at the next port.

Simple to act like an adult and behave. If your behavior is not up to par with the ship's security, you could be taken to the ship's brig (jail) and told to leave at the next port. Getting home will then be *your* responsibility.

Don't take a chance. Don't partake in a shouting match. Don't punch anybody. You will most likely be told to get off at the next port.

Again, if you do choose (and it is a choice) to be unruly or too drunk, there is a special place for you on the ship. And it is not your cabin! Those ship brigs are real!

H. THINGS TO DO ON BOARD YOUR SHIP

Please keep in mind all the activities I mention in this book are not on every ship. Ship's activities vary, depending on the cruise line.

Every evening when you get back to your room, you will have the next day's cruise newsletter waiting for you. In this newsletter you will find every show and every event taking place on the ship for the next day. You can easily plan out your day if you so choose.

The newsletter lists the arrival and departure of every port of call, when you can get off in port and when you need to be back on board your ship. You will also find ads for the ship's on-board shops.

These newsletters (also known as ship schedules) will keep you informed of exactly what you need to

Chapter 4 – LIFE ON BOARD THE SHIP

know. Your ship's schedule, emergency information for the ship, etcetera.

We take our newsletter with us everywhere we go. You will find the edge on some ship's newsletters is convenient for tearing off to take with you, but we take the whole thing.

The edge shows the schedule for the day, whereas the newsletter expands more and talks about the events for the day. We highlight what looks enticing to us (usually all of it).

If you forget your newsletter and leave it in your cabin, you can go by Guest Services and find a stack of them on the counter ready for you to grab.

Most cruise lines offer apps on your phone listing the day's information on it for your ship. Times in ports, what time you will arrive in your next port, what time you need to be back on your ship at the port, emergency information for the ship, etcetera.

Activities on the ship are ongoing, even on port days. If you choose not to do an excursion, no doubt you will have fun staying on board your ship!

Grab a glass of wine to sip on while watching the beautiful sunrise or sunset. How about listening to jazz at one of the on-board lounges? Or watching a beautiful sunset sitting in the Jacuzzi?

The hot tubs and pools are kept spotless by the staff.

Find a great book in the ship's library to enjoy while you relax. Or if you are more energetic, head to the fitness room where you will find all types of workout equipment. The views from the fitness room are awesome.

Don't forget your gym clothes if you plan to utilize the gym. If you are a fitness buff, they've got you covered.

Gyms are open 24 hours a day on most ships! Can't sleep? Head to the gym for a quiet workout!

More workout equipment than you can imagine as well as a jogging track on every ship!

The jogging track will be out in the open on the upper deck. I have utilized this on a few of our trips. As I get older, it becomes a walking track, not a jogging track!

You will also find yoga classes during the day. If cycling is your thing, they've got you covered with stationary cycling as well.

Chapter 4 – LIFE ON BOARD THE SHIP

You prefer water aerobics? You will find it on most every ship. There will be exercise classes, including Zumba and Pilates, on board. You can sign up for these at the gym area. Some of these classes may be an extra cost.

But why pay for exercise classes when you can get it for free simply by walking into the gym? Or do laps in the pool before fellow passengers wake in the mornings.

The cruise director will be certain there will be lots of game shows and contests on the ship. Join in the fun! In fact, volunteer to be one of the contestants. These activities are a blast!

Audience participation makes the games much more fun! Family Feud, Newlywed Game (always hilarious), Minute to Win It, just to name a few.

You will find activities galore around the pool area. We have seen a man's hairy chest contest, a belly flop contest as well as a man's best-looking legs contest. We've seen cannonball contests for the ladies. They're all pretty comical!

You may want to be sure your children are in the Kids' Club during these fun and crazy contests if you get easily offended.

Cruise Control

There are normally waterslides at several pools on the ship. Some of them are huge! There is a slide on one of the newest Royal Caribbean ships going out over the ocean! You will see adults as well as kiddos on these slides.

Royal Caribbean also has a large area on the back of some of their ships where the FlowRider provides tons of fun. This is where they teach you how to surf, either on your feet or on your stomach. Lots of fun!

On every ship we have been on, there has been an adults-only pool. So, if you're looking for a break from the little ones, send them to the Kids' Club and head to the adults-only pool.

With the exception of the Disney ships, most all other ships have casinos on board. As a general rule, the casinos are crowded. You'll meet a large number of your fellow cruisers here.

Some ships allow smoking in one-half of the casino, some don't allow any smoking.

Rock climbing walls are on most of the larger ships and most are free of charge. These walls are steep. You are, of course, strapped into a ship-provided harness and helmet. Looks fun, but we have never tried it.

Chapter 4 – LIFE ON BOARD THE SHIP

Many of the larger ships now have ice skating rinks. It is loads of fun sitting in the area watching others skate. It's honestly comical sometimes! Everyone is having fun!

Bowling alleys are on some of the larger ships as well. Also, comical and fun!

Your family may want to join in for the family talent show. Auditions are normally held close to the beginning of the cruise with the actual talent show occurring on one of the last evenings of the cruise.

This is a fun time for all and showcases some awesome talent! You will see people from all walks of life in this show.

There are all types of trivia games held every day. These are thoroughly fun. Name That Tune, Name That Celebrity, Name That Movie, and sports trivia are just a few of the great trivia games.

You are sure to walk away with more knowledge than you had when it started. These trivia games sometimes have great prizes!

You may find trivia tournaments on your cruise. And some of the answers are hilarious!

Cruise Control

You will find many types of classes on board. Scrapbooking, knitting, flower arranging, cooking, ballroom dancing, line dancing, Bible study, photography, and the like.

How about a jewelry-making class? You may find those on your ship as well. Supplies in these classes are usually free of charge.

We have even seen classes on learning the stock market. Personally, while I'm on vacation, I don't want to stress my brain out with numbers.

Scavenger hunts are always fun. These are most often held by the Kids' Club. They will go all over the ship looking for items.

Over the years, we have provided many items to the participating pre-teens and teens. Fun!

There are wine tastings on board some ships. The tastings are at no cost, and you will be able to purchase wines at discounted prices.

Many ships have wine cellars, champagne bars, and cigar bars.

Have you ever seen a robotic bartender? You will see them on Royal Caribbean's newest ships. Pretty cool to watch!

Chapter 4 – LIFE ON BOARD THE SHIP

The ice bars are fun to visit as well!

Also, on Royal Caribbean's newest ships, you may see a skydiving simulator, RipCord, right on deck. You will float on air inside a wind tunnel as if you are skydiving. This is free at the time of this writing on the Quantum Class ships of Royal Caribbean.

Some of the dinner theaters will have mystery dinners. A lot of fun to participate in. You enjoy a fabulous meal, all while figuring out Who Dun It.

Family movie time is customarily held on the giant outdoor screen in the pool area. Grab some chairs, and relax under the stars watching a great movie.

And don't forget the unlimited free popcorn they will have waiting for you!

There are ships providing indoor movie theaters as well as 4-D theaters. The movies are top-rated and suitable for adults and children.

You will find a piano bar on most ships. This is one of my favorite places to go on board. Most times the audience will sing along with the entertainer. Lots of fun!

<u>Cruise Control</u>

Karaoke is offered on most nights on the ship. If you love to belt it out, go try your hand at this. Why not? In all probability, you'll never see these people again anyway!

There are comedy clubs on most ships. These are always fun. They will have an adults-only show late at night.

You will find various types of music on board all around the ship. Jazz, Reggae, Latino, Motown, Easy Listening, Classical.

It will be playing at most hours of the day. And you can dance to all of it!

Table tennis and pool tables will be available on many ships. There will usually be one or two tables, so you may need to make a reservation if ping pong or shooting pool is your thing.

You may enjoy the crafting classes on many ships. This is a great way to get started in crafting if you've never tried it before.

You may see free classes in scrapbooking and jewelry making.

There is a video and arcade room on many ships. These are always fun. Many people spend hours in

Chapter 4 – LIFE ON BOARD THE SHIP

these recreation areas. You will likely find the teenagers in the arcade at most times of the day and evening.

Some ships have a separate room for laser tag for the little ones and teens. Well, adults enjoy this as well!

Go-karts, anyone? One of the newest additions to ships is go-karts. Or how about bumper cars? You'll find those on some ships as well. What a blast!

You will see chef's demonstrations while on board. This is always exciting and fun. My favorite demonstrations are the desserts! Too beautiful to eat.

We also enjoy the ice carvings and fruit carvings. These are beautiful!

Oftentimes, parades abound on cruise ships. You may see movie characters, Shrek, Cinderella, Big Bird. The adults as well as the little ones love these parades.

On the last ship we were on, there was a full-size, working carousel. Especially fun for the little ones.

Love to read but don't want to lug your own book around in your luggage? Grab one from the ship's library the first or second day on your cruise, and you'll be set for the rest of your trip.

The better books will go fast, so make sure you visit the library shortly after the ship sets sail.

Books weigh your luggage down anyway. Borrow the ship's!

In the library, you may also find free crossword puzzles, Sudoku and other types of fun puzzles or brain teasers.

Don't overlook the card room if you enjoy board games and card games. They're free as well.

There are Bible study classes on board many ships.

There are also group meetings for singles, the LGBTQ community, Friends of Bill W. (Alcoholics Anonymous), and many other various types of groups.

Keep in mind the show in the main theater is a different show every night with two different times each night. While showtimes vary on each ship, we have found showtimes to be around 8:00 p.m. and another at around 10:00 p.m.

Chapter 4 – LIFE ON BOARD THE SHIP

These are fabulous, live Broadway-type productions. You will see musicals, comedians, dancers, magicians, aerialists, hypnotists, and the like, all working together with the ship's superb live band.

The main shows are comparable to Vegas shows and are included in the ticket price for the cruise. Excellent shows! Go and enjoy!

Oftentimes, you will see these entertainers offer free workshops during the day. Want to learn how to juggle? Check out the workshop.

One of the shows may be a hilarious talent show put on by the ship's crew!

When you book your cruise, on many ships you can pre-book tickets to the shows if you choose to. These shows are free, but on many ships, you will need to reserve tickets.

If they are all booked up, you can always go to the show anyway because you may get the seats of the people with tickets who did not show up.

This is usually a large number of people. After all, you never truly know what you may be doing on a ship!

Be aware, there is no flash photography allowed in these shows.

If you miss an activity or show, no worries! You have a ship channel on your cabin television continually replaying everything happening on the ship.

You can see from the various activities there is no problem with having days at sea and finding things to do. You can relax or be busy with fun on the ship all day long.

People have downloaded episodes of their favorite binge-watching show on their laptops or tablets before leaving home. We have never done this as we are normally too busy being on the go. But there are people who prefer to rest and relax in their rooms. Or maybe they can't sleep!

I. GRATUITIES & TIPPING

I am putting this section on tipping in because I do not want you to get to the end of your cruise and not understand tips will be added to your shipboard account, also known as your closing bill.

Plus, you may want to include this cost when you budget for your cruise.

Chapter 4 – LIFE ON BOARD THE SHIP

Immensely important but often overlooked, tipping. On every ship we have been on, and I would venture to say all ships, the crew works non-stop, day and night, to make sure your cruise is the best of the best.

Many of the more luxurious, costly cruise lines, (Azamara, Seabourn, Silversea and others), do not allow tipping. These fees are built directly into the cost of the cruise.

When we first started cruising, the ship would provide tiny envelopes you would put your tips in for the various staff. Then you would run around the ship on the last day handing out these envelopes to the staff you wanted to be generous with.

These days, you will find your tips attached to your final bill at the end of your cruise. Unquestionably more convenient for passengers.

Tipping is not mandatory. You are at liberty to have these tips taken off of your bill at the end of your cruise, or to lower them to a smaller amount.

But why would you? A tip is a tiny expression of your gratitude for those crew members who went out of their way to make your trip fabulous.

Cruise Control

International travelers, especially from countries where tipping is not customary, may not understand tipping is part of the salary of these hardworking staff and crew members. Many of the staff and crew rely on these tips to garner a decent salary.

We have never considered tipping as extra. We include it in the total cost of our cruise because we appreciate how hard these people work.

Not only do we accept this tipping service charge added to our final bill, we tip crew members during our voyage who go above and beyond. And you will find staff who do this all over the ship. You will rarely see a staff member sitting down.

We bring plenty of dollar bills specifically to do this. If they provide us exemplary service, they receive exemplary tipping from us.

To be honest, we have never been on a ship where we wanted to complain due to poor service.

These employees are hard-working and deserve to be treated well and with respect. They make you believe you are the only person they are taking care of, and they deserve your appreciation.

Again, don't forget the people who handle your luggage for you. You pretty much do not have to do

Chapter 4 – LIFE ON BOARD THE SHIP

anything upon arriving at the dock for your ship's departure.

The amounts for gratuities attached to your bill will vary according to cruise line. If you are concerned, ask about this when you book your cruise.

The average amount as of this writing is $12-$14 per day per guest.

A gratuity of 15%-18% will be automatically added to any alcoholic drink from the bars. They will present you with a slip when you receive your drink, and the tip will be on there.

If you want to pay extra, you are free to add it on there. But keep in mind, the tip is *already on the bill*. Many people do not know this.

If you plan to frequent the same bar, if you do add extra tips, your service for the remainder of your cruise will be exemplary at the bar you frequent. They will remember you.

Spa services will have an automatic tip as well. You can, of course, adjust this tip, according to your service.

J. THANK YOUR CABIN STEWARD

All employees on a cruise ship work hard to make sure you have the time of your life.

The cabin steward is the one who makes your day in, day out life more pleasant in your cabin. They are constantly making sure your cabin is clean and everything is in its proper place.

Every day your cabin will look like you walked into it for the first time. Your bed will be made in the mornings and turned back in the evenings when your day is over and you are ready to go to bed.

He/she will likely make a cute towel animal to leave on your bed or hang from your light. These always make me smile!

The steward is call to bring you anything you need. They are a call away and are prompt, working diligently to attend to your needs.

If you put your Do Not Disturb sign on the door, don't forget to remove it when you leave. You may come back to an untidy cabin if you forget to take it down.

I must have our cabin tidy, simply because I can't stand clutter. So, I make sure the cabin is tidy and

Chapter 4 – LIFE ON BOARD THE SHIP

things are put away before we walk out of the cabin door. This helps the steward clean the cabin better and quicker too.

If you make an effort to leave your cabin in order when you leave for the day, your steward will notice this and provide you even better service. It only takes a minute to tidy up.

Greet them, ask them how their day is going. Thank them often for the wonderful job they are doing to make sure all your needs are met.

Many guests will contemplate ways to show their appreciation to their steward.

Make them a small gift basket before you ever leave home with small toiletries included. Get them a gift card at one of the ports as they will likely be going back to the same ports on the next sailing. Bring them candy bars or bags of snacks.

If you leave a small token of appreciation on the last day of the cruise, be sure to put their name on it so they will know it's for them.

We sometimes tip them at the beginning of our cruise, as we believe this makes for even better service.

Cruise Control

These guys are in the business of helping, and they have a strong desire to make sure you do not have a need for anything while on your cruise.

A great way to say thank you to your cabin steward is to send a note to the director of the cruise. Mention your cabin steward's name or any other exemplary crew member's name. Express your gratitude for this person who helped to make your trip so enjoyable.

You may receive a survey from the cruise line after your cruise. Fill it out. Mention your steward or any other crew member by name and comment on how well they took care of you.

Learn their name on the first day of your cruise, and call them by name each and every time you see them. They will give you above and beyond type of service.

On the last cruise we went on, I took several thank-you cards to give to staff who were extra helpful. I gave one to our steward along with a gift set of small toiletries. He was truly grateful. Lets them know how much you appreciate them.

Chapter 4 – LIFE ON BOARD THE SHIP

If your steward is especially helpful, you might consider leaving them an additional tip on the last evening of your cruise.

Chapter 5 – DEBARKATION

A. SETTLING YOUR ON-BOARD ACCOUNT

On many ships, you can settle your on-board account on your television. If you have no need to visit the Guest Services' desk on the morning of debarkation, paying on your television is much quicker.

If you have no questions about your account, they will put your final amount due on the credit card you provided, and there is no need to visit the Guest Services' desk.

If you supplied cash, you will need to visit Guest Services to either receive the cash you may have left, or you will need to supply more cash.

If you are new to cruising and are confused about the debarkation process, you will find a channel on the TV outlining the steps.

B. DEBARKATION OF LUGGAGE

On the last night of your cruise, you will pack your belongings and place your luggage out in the hallway around 7:00 p.m. and no later than around 11:00 p.m.

Cruise Control

The porters will leave colored luggage tags corresponding with your departure time in your cabin for you to attach to your luggage. These tags are used to call guests to debark (by their certain luggage tag color). The tags also help keep things running in an orderly fashion.

You will use these same colored tags to claim your luggage in the cruise terminal.

If you have a flight to catch and your designated time to debark the ship is not adequate, simply go to the Guest Services' desk and ask for another time.

All the luggage will be gathered from the hallways during the night. It will then be at the terminal for you to retrieve when you debark the next morning.

When you pack your luggage the night before departure, don't forget to keep the clothes and shoes out you will wear the next morning for debarkation. Some cruisers wear the same clothes they had on the previous night. Also, don't pack your toiletries you will need.

You can have your luggage taken directly to the airport for an extra nominal fee. Many people

Chapter 5 – DEBARKATION

believe it is worth it to not have to deal with luggage, especially if you have a large family traveling.

We have not seen many people do this, but if you prefer, you are allowed to carry your own bags off the ship upon debarkation. Of course, if you do this, you will have no waiting during the debarkation process.

If you have a flight to catch, carrying your own luggage off will allow you to head straight to customs, straight to the airport. The longer you wait, the busier the taxis will be.

Again, when you debark the ship, you will exit to a terminal with thousands of pieces of luggage. It is a great idea to mark your luggage in order for you to easily locate it.

You will be told what specific area to go to for your luggage. But if you have it marked, you will be able to quickly and easily spot it.

C. DEBARKATION OF PASSENGERS

The ships we've been on have always arrived to home port between 7:00 a.m. and 8:00 a.m. The captain must receive clearance from the port authority before debarkation can occur.

Cruise Control

As it is difficult to hear the PA system in your cabin, we always go to a public area (like the buffet for breakfast) on the morning of debarkation so we can hear what is being announced.

On debarkation morning, keep in mind the crew only has a couple hours to get the entire ship ready for the next cruise leaving in the afternoon.

Clear out of your cabin in a timely manner, waiting in one of the common areas to debark from the ship.

Breakfast will be available in several areas of the ship during the debarkation process.

The crew will request you depart your cabin by 8:30-9:00 a.m. on the last day. You will wait in your designated deboarding area. The information for where you should wait will be in your cabin the night before.

I know, we all hate when our cruise ends! But it is common courtesy to be considerate of the passengers arriving for the next cruise so they can have as much fun as you've had.

You will need your cruise card one last time to exit the ship. Don't forget to take it with you as you head to the gangway.

Chapter 5 – DEBARKATION

Again, debarkation will not begin until after the ship has been cleared by Immigration and Customs. The color of the luggage tags your steward left in your cabin the previous night will be called to exit the ship. Then another color and so on.

After you depart the ship, you will take a ramp to Immigration and Customs, one line for U.S. residents and one line for non-U.S. residents.

Be respectful with these people. They have thousands of people to release. Have your passport ready.

We have found this process does not take long. We have never seen any problems with the debarkation process, though I'm sure they exist.

One more word of caution. If you spent any time in the casino, be sure to cash your chips in or anything else you have pertaining to the casino as you will not be able to after departing the ship.

CONCLUSION

So, there you have it. Our way of making the most of a floating city where all you have to worry about is what kind of food you want to eat or what site you want to see.

I hope I have captured the beauty of cruising and how much fun it can be! It will be what you choose for it to be.

Cruising is positively a luxury vacation, but it does not have to be expensive. Plan your trip carefully, and you will not break the bank.

You might even find yourself addicted to cruising!

I hope you have enjoyed this book and gleaned a ton of information sure to help make your cruise vacation the best ever!

Happy and safe cruising!

AUTHOR'S REQUEST

Thank you for taking time to read this book. Hopefully, you will be one of the most informed passengers on your cruise!

If this book has benefitted you, please leave a review for it on Amazon.com. The stars readers give books and the reviews they provide help other readers decide whether or not the book is a suitable fit for them.

It takes a couple minutes to leave a review. You do not even have to use your name. You can do it anonymously.

Your help means so much to myself and other readers who may benefit from reading this book.

Thanks so much!

I can be reached at:
www.justperfectlyimperfect.com.

ABOUT THE AUTHOR

Robin Gail's favorite way to vacation is cruising! She has enjoyed cruising for over 20 years.

Robin was born in and grew up in Fort Worth, Texas. She attended court reporting college and passed her state exam to become a Certified Court Reporter by the Supreme Court of the State of Texas.

After college, she spent the next 30 years as a practicing court reporter. Her entrepreneurial efforts began one year after being certified. She started her own court reporting company and has continued to be self-employed, working successfully at home for 29 years.

In 2017, Robin Gail became an Amazon #1 bestselling author after publishing Dementia or Alzheimer's?, a non-fiction book detailing her and her husband's efforts of caring for her mother in her mother's courageous battle living with this disease.

Robin loves to learn new things and is an avid reader of both fiction and non-fiction. She enjoys gardening, playing the piano, planning parties, cooking, photography, and writing.

She can be reached at: robin@justperfectlyimperfect.com.

REFERENCES

www.vacationstogo.com

www.bookingbuddy.com

www.cruisemates.com

www.cruisecritic.com

www.carnival.com

www.royalcaribbean.com

www.princess.com

www.hollandamerica.com

www.celebritycruises.com

www.disneycruise.disney.go.com

www.cruisecomplete.com

www.weather.com

www.travel.state.gov

Made in the USA
Monee, IL
17 January 2023